ASK THE RIGHT QUESTIONS, HIRE THE BEST PEOPLE
Fourth Edition

RON FRY
Best-selling author of
101 Great Answers to the Toughest Interview Questions

CAREER
PRESS
The Career Press, Inc.

This edition first published in 2010 by Career Press, an imprint of
Red Wheel/Weiser, LLC
With offices at:
65 Parker Street, Suite 7
Newburyport, MA 01950
www.redwheelweiser.com
www.careerpress.com

ISBN: 978-1-63265-130-3

Library of Congress Cataloging-in-Publication Data
Fry, Ronald W.
    Ask the right questions, hire the best people / by Ron Fry. --3rd ed.
        p. cm.
    Includes index.
    ISBN 978-1-63265-130-3
    ISBN 978-1-60163-750-5
    1. Employee selection. 2. Employment interviewing. 3. Prediction of
occupational success. I. Title.

HF5549.5.S38F79 2010
658.3'1124--dc22
2009050334

Cover design by Howard Grossman/12E Design
Cover photos by Africa Studio/shutterstock
Interior by Gina Schenck
Typeset in Minion Pro

Printed in Canada
MAR
10 9 8 7 6 5 4 3 2 1

Contents

INTRODUCTION 5

CHAPTER 1
DEFINE THE JOB 15

CHAPTER 2
EFFECTIVE SCREENING TECHNIQUES 27

CHAPTER 3
TYPES OF INTERVIEWS 37

CHAPTER 4
HERE WE GO 49

CHAPTER 5
TELL ME A LITTLE ABOUT YOURSELF 69

CHAPTER 6
QUESTIONS ABOUT THEIR EDUCATION   93

CHAPTER 7
QUESTIONS ABOUT THEIR WORK EXPERIENCE   107

CHAPTER 8
QUESTIONS ABOUT STYLE AND SUBSTANCE   125

CHAPTER 9
QUESTIONS ABOUT CORE COMPETENCIES   139

CHAPTER 10
QUESTIONS ABOUT THE MOST RECENT JOB   157

CHAPTER 11
QUESTIONS FOR MANAGERS AND EXECUTIVES   177

CHAPTER 12
QUESTIONS TO DISCOVER HIDDEN OBJECTIONS   189

CHAPTER 13
AVOIDING ILLEGAL QUESTIONS   205

CHAPTER 14
WRAP IT UP   213

INDEX   221

INTRODUCTION

This is the fourth edition of *Ask the Right Questions, Hire the Best People*, the corollary to *101 Great Answers to the Toughest Interview Questions,* which is now in its seventh edition. I wrote the first edition of the latter nearly 30 years ago. It continues to sell thousands of copies, year after year. Why has it done so well for so long? It's simple, straightforward, practical, and written in a welcoming and humorous style. And it has clearly helped millions of candidates prepare for *you*.

But this book is for *you*. You may think that changing circumstances significantly affect your approach to interviewing: Unemployment goes up and down, the economy grows and contracts, companies and whole industries bloom or wither. Whatever the overall economic environment or the particular state of your own company's fortunes, the rudiments of good interviewing—and the tools you need to effectively and efficiently separate superior from unsatisfactory candidates—have changed surprisingly little.

No matter how many questions I have supplied—and there are hundreds—you are really just posing variations of the same *six* questions:

1. *Can the candidate do the job?* Does he have the specific qualifications you are seeking? The right degree? Pertinent experience? Appropriate skills and competencies?

2. *Will he or she do the job better than the other people you are interviewing or considering?* Can she *prove* that by supplying great answers to your questions and asking equally detailed questions of her own?

3. *Will the candidate actually accept the job if offered?* How much does he want this specific job? Or is he just desperate to take *any* job...even this one?

4. *Will the candidate, no matter how sterling his or her credentials, fit in with the rest of the group?* The smaller the company or department, the more important this "chemistry" question may be to you. In a one- or two-person office, it may be a primary concern. You want to avoid becoming so dazzled by a candidate's qualifications that you fail to assess how she will fit in with your company culture.

5. *Will the candidate make me look like a genius or a fool?* I assume you have superiors who will question your judgement if too many of your new hires fail to make the grade. You failures as an interviewer may wind up slashing your bonus, killing a promotion, and even jeopardizing your own job.

6. *What is the candidate going to cost me in money, time, and effort?* How long before he actually starts contributing to the bottom line? And what will it cost you to get him there?

Of course, if you could just ask every candidate these six questions and easily identify the winners, you wouldn't need this book! But if you have spent any time at all interviewing, you know it doesn't work that way. So you *do* need me.

I believe this new edition will help *you* as much as its counterpart has helped your potential employees. And it contains *more* than enough questions for you to consider. The competition for *Ask the Right Questions* includes books touting 96, 201, 501, and 701 questions to ask. One book has 60 straight pages of nothing *but* questions! What good are such lists if you aren't told what answers you're trying to elicit?

Whatever your experience, company size, interviewing style, or the number or type of candidates you are seeking, I firmly believe you will learn how to confidently and successfully conduct *any* interview with the help of this book.

An organized layout to get you organized

Chapters 1, 2, and 3 (and the first part of Chapter 4) explain what you need to do and think about before you talk to any candidates. From developing cogent and effective job descriptions to types of interviews, from how to handle a candidate who shows up an hour late to suffering through a "Silent Cal" or "Verbose Victor." After you study these first chapters, you *will* be prepared.

In the second part of Chapter 4 and Chapters 5 through 14, we'll get into the meat of the book—the questions you should ask and the answers you should expect to hear.

I've formatted the book in a way that makes it most practical and easy to use. Each question is followed by one or more subheadings. For example:

What do you want to hear? (What information should the question elicit?)

 (What's a good answer?)

 (What's a poor answer?)

There may be follow-up questions or those you can substitute (variations) after each as well.

Thumbs down probably means "thank you and good-bye"

Many readers have told me the "thumbs down" remarks are the most helpful part of the book, because they clearly indicate when you should just consider thanking the candidate and moving on. These are answers that would make most interviewers cringe.

After almost every question in the book, I could have included the same list of general cautions: those factors that should give you pause after any question…or in any interview. So as not to unnecessarily clutter up the book, let me just state these all-encompassing negatives right here:

You meant 8 o'clock in the morning?

Many interviewers will simply cancel (and not reschedule) an interview if the candidate is late. It doesn't matter that traffic backed up, his cat threw up a hairball, or he just got lost in your building. Being on time is not racing into the reception area with moments to spare. A prepared candidate should be at least 15 minutes early.

Somehow I knew it was you

I react negatively to candidates wearing too much perfume or cologne, more makeup than a runway model, an armload of bangles and bells, or sporting a 5 o'clock shadow…at 9 a.m. You may be more or less forgiving.

First impressions *are* important and your initial gut reaction to a candidate *is* a valid one, so if you *immediately* sense an interview would be a waste of your (valuable) time, you are free to make an excuse and cancel it then and there.

Do you actually dress like that every day?

No matter how "loose" and unstructured your corporate culture, I would question the seriousness of a candidate sporting any attire you consider unprofessional or inappropriate.

Do you mind if I call my mother for advice?

There should be a new reality series featuring the bizarre behavior of some interviewees, as they chew, burp, scratch, swear, cry, laugh, and scream their way into our hearts. Interviewees have shown up drunk or stoned, brought their mothers with them, fallen asleep, and even gone to the bathroom and never returned. Keeping a cell phone on during the interview is inappropriate. Actually receiving or making a call is bizarre.

If you are confronted by a candidate demonstrating these behaviors, you will not be blamed if you wonder, "If this is an example of his *best* behavior, what (*gasp!*) do I have to look forward to?"

Lies, lies, and damned lies

Checking references is vital. While some candidates may "fudge" their credentials here and there, the number of candidates who brazenly lie about where and when they worked, what they did, and/or where and when (or even if) they attended college, has skyrocketed. One resume-writing service estimated that nearly half of the resumes they vetted contained serious inaccuracies.

No matter how lowly the job, there are significant expenses involved with hiring someone to perform it, so you must take the time to check out references. And the higher up the food chain the job, the more intensive your scrutiny must be.

Lacking a particular skill or experience may not automatically exclude someone from getting the job. Lying about it should. Just be aware that the litigious nature of our society has made reference-checking a challenge. Many companies have instructed managers to merely confirm a former employee's salary, date of hire, and date of separation, with*out* revealing any negative aspects of his or her time there or, even worse, if and why he or she was fired.

If someone is fabricating a lot of his or her experience, the questions in this book will help you separate the occasional truths from the plethora of lies.

Thank you for sharing. Now please stop!

Although honesty may be the best (and only) policy, you may be taken aback if a candidate is a little *too* confiding; anything she does in the privacy of her own home is not something you need to hear about.

Some candidates will make your job decidedly easy because of their tendency to blurt out the truth. When I asked one woman what interested her about a job opening, she responded, "Heck, I just need a job with benefits. I owe way too much on my credit cards."

No Debbie Downers

A candidate should attempt to make every minute of his interview a positive experience. In my mind, someone who complains about his last job, boss, duties, or even the elevator ride upstairs is not someone *I* want to hire.

Uh, look over here please

To many interviewers, a candidate's inability to "look them in the eye" indicates she has something to hide; so does being overly fidgety or nervous. You should expect a promising candidate to greet you with a firm handshake, sit straight up and, of course, look you in the eye. (There is always an exception to the rule: I hired an experienced acquisitions editor to head a department despite his near-constant hand-rubbing during our interview. Sometimes nervous behavior is just...nerves.)

Likewise, you should be seeking people who are enthusiastic about what they do, so a candidate who sighs, looks out the window, or checks her watch during an interview may not fit the bill.

Study the candidate's body language. Although many people don't mean what they say or say what they mean, their non-verbal actions reveal *exactly* what they're feeling. According to studies, *more than half* of what we are trying to communicate is being received non-verbally.

He might be a trifle too confident

A candidate once said to me, barely five minutes into our interview, "I've got three other offers right now. What can you do for me?"

I helpfully showed him the door.

Yes, you are seeking confident, enthusiastic, and cheerful (and brave and clean and reverent...) candidates, but be wary of those who are too "over the top."

"Uh, why do you want to know?"

If you ask a simple question and a candidate starts to sweat, hems and haws, then tries to change the subject, you are free to wonder what she is hiding. Because if she isn't hiding anything, why is she acting so defensively?

"What does this company do?"

A key part of the interview process is preparation: researching the company, industry, and position, preparing pertinent questions, and nimbly sprinkling that knowledge into the conversation. So you should seriously question the commitment of a candidate who demonstrates a lack of such preparation. I *have* had candidates ask me what exactly my company did.

"Sure, Greg, you can have another lobster."

An interview over lunch is an excellent way to get a candidate to reveal aspects of his personality or behavior you want to know about, even if it's just whether Mom taught him manners. An otherwise-attractive candidate may seem decidedly less so after blithely ordering the most expensive item on the menu or inelegantly slurping spaghetti or soup.

"And then I worked for...oops!"

Throughout this book, I have attempted to give you the ability to formulate questions to elicit what you *really* want to know. The best answers are those that are most responsive to your stated (or unstated) needs. Because these answers should be "customized" to match the candidate's qualifications with your company's needs, it's often difficult, if not impossible, to say that a particular answer is "right" or "wrong." But some answers *are* clearly wrong:

◄ Any answer, no matter how articulate and specific, that fails to actually answer the question asked.

◄ Any answer that reveals that the candidate is unqualified for the job.

◄ Any answer that provides information that doesn't jibe with a candidate's resume and/or cover letter.

◄ Any answer that reveals an inability to take responsibility for failures/weaknesses/bad decisions/bad results, or that tries to take full credit for a project to which others clearly contributed.

Although you may not consider any of these an automatic reason for immediate dismissal, an accumulation of two or more should give you pause. Some, like dishonesty, should make you do more than just pause.

Setting up your interview plan

The questions in this book are loosely grouped by type. They are not in some suggested order. So read the entire book and then decide, on a case-by-case basis, which questions to ask (and in what order) as you approach each candidate. And don't forget Chapter 13, which covers the illegal and ill-advised questions you *don't* want to ask.

Finally, a word about the usage of gender throughout this book: I've chosen to mix up the usage of "he" and "she" or "him" and "her" and avoided awkward "he or she" constructions when necessary.

Rather than spend a lot more time telling you what you're going to learn, let's just get you started. Good luck!

Ron Fry
November, 2017

1

DEFINE THE JOB

Some interviewers fool themselves into believing that they can improvise their way to a successful hire with little or no preparation. I don't think you can. The cost of hiring an employee today is higher than ever, and poor hires have a way of affecting the careers of the managers responsible for them. That means *you*.

The hard truth is that hiring the right person for any job takes a lot of work, both before and during the interview. It is not just a function of asking the right questions *during* the interview, but also spending the time to prepare *before* the interview. Although such preparatory work is not that difficult to complete, my sense is that it's routinely ignored by too many employers, especially small-company managers. Such interviewers "wing it"—and then wonder why the person they hired either didn't work out or quickly left to take advantage of another opportunity.

What is this job, anyway?

You'll find it difficult to evaluate applicants, much less attract and retain good people, if you haven't established a clear and concise set of requirements for the job.

Is your organization experiencing high turnover in a particular position? If so, it's entirely possible that the job is poorly defined or the components of the job description are totally incongruous. (Another possibility, of course, is that you have *no* written job description for employees to use as a starting point, in which case you should expect continued personnel headaches.)

One entrepreneur I know told me of a job she once tried to fill whose duties included the following:

◄ Conducting regular meetings with key vendors.

◄ Evaluating quotes and references from new vendors.

◄ Making critical marketing strategy recommendations.

◄ Managing the inventory in a 5,000-square-foot warehouse.

◄ Composing initial drafts of flyer and catalog copy.

◄ Analyzing cash-flow predictions.

◄ Filling in for telemarketing staff when absences arose.

Do you see a problem here? Six different hires in an equal number of months certainly did. None lasted longer than a few weeks; one failed to return after lunch...on his second day.

The various elements of the job were so wildly out of balance—and required such varied skills and training—that no one could have reasonably believed they belonged to a single position.

As a result, no matter how accomplished a new hire, he or she quickly felt overwhelmed, overworked, and underpaid.

One of the initial keys to hiring the right person for the job is to make sure it is *a* job, not a series of disparate tasks that would tax anyone's spectrum of skills, no matter how broad.

There are undoubtedly times when a dynamic company needs to ask employees to "pinch hit" in areas outside their daily routine. But there has to *be* a daily routine from which to deviate! Before you try to find the "perfect person" for your "perfect job," take a long, hard look at exactly what that job will mean to the person who will spend the majority of his or her waking hours performing it.

If your job offers no defining, consistent sense of purpose, you will find it difficult to attract an applicant who will perform it well over an extended period of time. "Revolving door" positions cost your company money. In most workplaces, asking the company "Renaissance person" to sweep up or punch endless reams of figures into a computer system is an expensive mistake that will inevitably leave someone (probably you) in permanent "search mode."

Remember: They are not you

Here's an important reminder for entrepreneurs and others who have personal stakes in their organizations: *You* may well be willing to wake up early, stay late, and do anything—repeat, *anything*—to meet your company's goals. You may *have* to scrub toilets *and* crunch numbers *and* pack shipments *and* make sales calls *and...and....* But you *chose* your bed—you *have* to sleep in it and pay for it.

As a fellow entrepreneur, I applaud your dedication, zeal, and crazy belief that you will, of course, defy all odds and actually succeed.

At the same time, you should be aware that many candidates will not share your enthusiasm to do anything, anywhere, any time.

If you want an accountant, create a job description that focuses on accounting work. If you want a salesperson, the job description should focus on sales work. If, however, you want someone who will pay any price as an accountant, bear any burden as a salesperson, and share your personal willingness to peel dried chewing gum from beneath tables at 11 p.m. on a Saturday night, you're going to have a problem. You're not looking for an employee; you're looking for a kindred spirit. You may have to wait awhile before you find one. And, when you do, you may have to give up a piece of your company to compensate him or her for the overweening dedication you expect.

Identify irrelevant components of the job. Then be honest about what duties and responsibilities should remain in the job description and which should be reassigned to someone else. Share your conclusions with others in the organization and get their input. Don't stop tinkering until you've developed a workable job description that's both coherent and well-organized around a central theme. Remember: The fact that you are (or would be) willing to perform any given task in the description will not be persuasive to an employee who ends up feeling pulled in a dozen different directions at once. Make it your goal to avoid hiring applicants who (secretly) plan to stay with you only until a better opportunity arises.

Next, do a little brainstorming about the background, experience, and skills your ideal candidate should bring to the table. Use the following questions as a starting point:

◄ What kind of educational background is required?

◄ What level of computer experience is required?

- ◄ What specific software tools are required?

- ◄ What other technical skills are required?

- ◄ What business background should the applicant have?

- ◄ What communication skills are required to fulfill the tasks associated with this position?

- ◄ How important are problem-solving skills in this position?

- ◄ What kinds of day-to-day challenges will the successful employee need to routinely overcome?

Pay particular attention to the specificity of each of the job duties listed.

As you work to develop and refine the job description, remember the old punch line: "Forgive me for writing you such a long letter. I didn't have time to write a short one." Make sure your job descriptions are both comprehensible and concise. Yes, it may take time (and, in larger organizations, a certain amount of political skill) to finalize a cogent, powerful description that includes the essentials of the job. But it will be time well spent.

If you don't work with the people in your organization to devise a job description that clearly sets out a range of related, interconnected responsibilities, you will almost inevitably end up hiring someone who abandons your organization the moment a better opportunity comes along. A "hit-and-run" hire will cost your company money, and it certainly won't reflect well on the person who interviewed the fast-disappearing candidate! Again, that would be you.

Ideally, your job description should outline duties that are consistent with the life and career goals of a particular applicant—the right applicant.

Remember: People work for a number of reasons, not just money. Job satisfaction is a big part of the equation. Personal rewards and fulfillment must be taken into account, and the requirements of the job must be perceived as congruent, tangible, and realistic by job seekers and employees alike. Ask yourself: Will the person *want* to fulfill the requirements of the position you've designed? Why?

Regardless of the level or nature of the position, a well-focused job description proves to the applicant that someone has taken the time to actually think about what needs to be done and who is needed to do it.

Give applicants a sense of your "corporate culture"

Is your organization a creative new startup? An industry-leading behemoth? A nonprofit organization with a sense of mission that all its employees share? Paint a brief portrait of your company, and let your potential hires know what kind of culture they'll be joining. This really can make a difference in the quality of applicants you attract and the success of those you hire. Why was someone with the required educational background and all the pertinent skills fired before he even got his ID tag? The answer usually involves some problem with how he "fit" in the organization.

Similarly, you should make an effort to give her some sense of what the daily routine is likely to look and feel like. Is the environment fast-paced? Is quality control an obsession for people in this department? Are you looking for someone who brings a high level of creativity to the workplace?

In addition to the traditional emphasis on educational, experience, and technical requirements, don't neglect to consider and include the particular "key competencies" necessary for success in that position. These may include anything from empathy and prudent risk-taking to communication, team-building, and/or customer-focused skills.

What to look for in the resumes you receive

If you have posted and advertised an attractive job opening, you may receive far more resumes than you ever expected. If the economy is relatively poor or the unemployment rate high, you may still receive a blizzard of resumes for even the *least* attractive openings.

If you work for a large organization, you are probably using an applicant tracking system to scan resumes for keywords and phrases to identify the few candidates you want to interview on the phone, via Skype, or in person. If you are still manually sifting through all the resumes that land on your doorstep or in your email—and you have my sympathy—there is a method to quickly and efficiently review them.

First, review the job description you composed earlier and refresh your memory. Go through the list of requirements and competencies you established. Remind yourself which elements you consider absolutely essential. Then "buzz" those resumes.

That's right—I said "buzz" them, not "read" them. One of the most enduring fictions of the world of employment is that prospective employers are under some moral compunction to actually read every stultifying word of the resumes they receive.

A resume is a document prepared for your convenience. As far as you're concerned, it has one purpose only: to make it easier for you to remove people from consideration. So look for the keywords that will prove a candidate has what you're seeking. Resumes that pass this initial test stay "in." Resumes that fail are "out."

This first step will probably remove from consideration a large chunk of the resumes on your desk—typically between 50 and 80 percent of them. Of the resumes that remain, some may have made a more positive impression on you than others. There are two likely reasons for this. First, the applicant may have taken the time and trouble to compose the resume and cover letter specifically to fit the opening you've advertised or posted. Second, the applicant may have work or educational experience that is particularly appropriate or competencies that are right on the money—a potential sign of a good match.

Place a small check mark in the upper-right hand corner of any resume that catches your eye for either of these reasons.

Give yourself a break of at least a couple of hours before you review the "in" pile again. When you start your review, look at each resume a little more closely than you did the first time. Read each resume once, and make notes in the margins as you proceed.

What exactly are you looking for? Beyond the formal requirements of the job, you want applicants whose resumes demonstrate confidence, enthusiasm, experience, and dependability.

Here's a strategy you can use to identify those qualities. Focusing only on the resumes in your "in" pile, and focusing *first* on the resumes that bear a check mark, *add* one check mark to the resume you're reading for every "yes" answer you can give to the following questions.

Be sure to apply the questions to both the resume *and* the cover letter. Many exceptional candidates will use the cover letter to amplify relevant experience. Reading the cover letter carefully may also give you immediate exposure to communication strengths (or weaknesses) not immediately evident in the resume.

◄ *Does the applicant make reference to at least one relevant success story that matches the requirements of the position, as you've identified them?* Past success in a similar situation indicates a good chance of success in the position you're trying to fill.

◄ *Do the person's qualifications mirror the background of an employee who has previously performed at a superior level in this position?* A profile that favorably compares with that of a top performer in your organization is worth reviewing closely. Keep an eye out for parallel educational accomplishments, similar career progress, even comparable leisure activities that support workplace performance.

◄ *Do educational and/or training credentials appear to be above average for this position?* Consider not only prestigious colleges and exemplary grade point averages, but also any references to professional seminars, workplace training, and other signs of commitment to personal and professional development.

◄ *Is the sequence of jobs or study clear and comprehensible, with no unexplained employment/education gaps during the previous five years?* Some resumes are designed to emphasize relevant skills and experience or pertinent competencies over chronology. This can make it difficult to evaluate the person's recent career path and overall dependability. If a candidate's resume has effectively camouflaged his recent past, but you want to interview him anyway, be sure to ask for a detailed, chronological work history early on. Be wary of unexplained gaps.

◄ *Is the resume and/or cover letter impressively creative or unusually well-executed?* People who creatively try to win your attention in a tasteful and compelling way may be above-average problem-solvers. They may take a similarly resourceful approach to other problems that come their way. Feel free, however, to discard any resumes that come taped to pepperoni pizza boxes…with or without the pie.

Now make an X in another corner of the resume for every "yes" answer to the following questions. Again, be sure to include both the resume *and* cover letter:

◄ *Are there obvious typographical or grammatical errors?* If the applicant can't be bothered to spell your name or your company's name correctly, or to appeal to someone for help in constructing a coherent sentence, there could be a problem with attention to detail in a workplace setting. Don't underestimate the importance of care and accuracy in this area. Given the availability of computerized spell-checkers and the incessant urging of innumerable career counselors, articles, and books to triple check for errors, there's simply no excuse for such sloppiness.

◄ *Does the applicant use the resume or cover letter as an opportunity to complain or assign blame— for anything?* This can be a very dangerous sign. Beware of applicants who didn't make the effort to optimistically approach challenging situations when constructing their resumes or cover letters.

◄ *Are any of the applicant's claims obviously overstated?* People who stretch the truth on their resumes and cover letters will probably stretch the truth in other situations. There's a difference between putting the best possible "spin" on an experience and outright lying. If you know or strongly suspect that the person's resume contains a statement that falls into the second category, "X" it.

◄ *Is the resume itself difficult to follow?* Resumes and cover letters are miniature tests of one's ability to convey important information concisely and effectively. If the document fails this test, "X" it.

Once you've asked each of these questions about all the resumes and cover letters in your "in" pile, you should have a group of resumes with checks and X marks on them. Then:

◄ Take any correspondence that has *even one* X mark and place it in your "out" pile for now. You can always re-evaluate your decisions later. At the moment, your aim is to focus on candidates whose credentials and presentation are exemplary.

◄ Take any correspondence that has no marks whatsoever and place it in a new pile, your "backup" pile. These are people you may choose to contact later if your top choices don't pan out.

◄ Take the remaining correspondence and place it in descending order, with the candidates who have the most check marks at the top of the pile.

Congratulations! You have already culled a stack of resumes into a reasonable number of candidates you actually want to interview. What form should that interview take? And how should you initiate contact with the applicant? You'll find those answers in the next chapter.

2

EFFECTIVE SCREENING TECHNIQUES

Simply calling all the people in your pile of top-tier resumes to ask some initial questions and set up in-person interviews is probably a waste of that most precious resource: time. Many applicants are skillful writers (or know skillful writers willing to prepare resumes and cover letters for them). Often, however, the person presented on paper will bear little relation to the flesh-and-blood human being it purports to describe.

Before you make the investment in time and energy to meet with anyone face-to-face, call and chat, either by phone or video (Skype). Give yourself the chance to evaluate the confidence, enthusiasm, experience, and dependability of your most promising leads.

If you're committed to using your time effectively, then you are obliged to regard the initial call as a screening interview, rather than simply a means of setting an appointment. For this interview (in fact, for *any* employment interview), you should be prepared to ask four types of questions:

◄ *Rapport questions.* These are questions that allow you to build interpersonal bridges with the candidate. They typically occur early on in the discussion and are meant to encourage the candidate to feel comfortable with you and, by extension, with your company. ("Hi, Bob. How are you doing today?")

◄ *Open-ended questions.* These questions allow the candidate a great deal of leeway in describing what he or she does best. ("Can you tell me about a time when you were really proud of what you did at Acme Company?")

◄ *Probing questions.* These questions focus on particular skills related to specific workplace experiences or decisions. ("Can you tell me what steps you took after the blackout to make sure that every department was prepared for a future emergency?"). These kinds of questions will help reveal inconsistencies, even untruths, including situations in which the candidate took credit for others' solutions or results.

◄ *Questions that aren't questions.* This is your chance to put the candidate at ease by giving gentle but clear instructions, rather than asking pointed queries. It takes some practice, but it's very effective at getting candidates to open up: *"What would help me most would be to learn what you felt was your most important experience as a young stockbroker. Please take a moment and think of an event from your early years at Cadwell House that you feel shaped your career in an important way. When you're ready, share that experience with me."*

The opening of your phone screen could sound like this:

You: *Mike Jones?*

Applicant: *Yes?*

You: *Hi, Mike. This is Mary Sweeney at Consolidated Widgets. You'd sent your resume over to us last week in response to our post on Indeed.com for an experienced widget inspector?*

Applicant: *Oh, right, right…*

You: *I was hoping I could talk to you for a few minutes. I'm glad we were able to connect.* **(rapport question)** *How are you?*

Applicant: *I'm fine. I'm really happy you called!*

You: *Well, that's great to hear. I hope I haven't caught you at a bad time.* **(rapport question)** *Have you got a few minutes right now, or should we schedule another call? It's fine if you want to set up another time.*

In most business settings, this is regarded as an extremely weak way to open a conversation, because it leaves the other person a clear opportunity to say, "Actually, I'm right in the middle of something just now." In this setting, however, that's exactly what you want to do: give the other person an opportunity to get off the phone.

Some applicants are so nervous receiving an unexpected call from a prospective employer that their responses are virtually meaningless. They need a chance to get their bearings. By opening the conversation in this way, you give the candidate a chance to soothe the butterflies that have suddenly taken up residence in his stomach. Be prepared to schedule another time or, at the very least, give the applicant a moment to track down that resume, take a deep breath, and make a good impression.

The applicant will either suggest setting up a new time to talk with you or let the conversation continue. Whichever the case, you'll want to make a little small talk, then move directly into a few basic questions to get a better sense of what motivates the person you're talking to:

You (rapport question): *So you live in Cambridge?*

Applicant: *Yes, I've been here for about eight years now.*

You (rapport question): *Do you have an apartment there?*

Applicant: *Yes, right off Central Square, next to the super-market. Do you know the area?*

You: *I sure do. As a matter of fact, about three years ago, I had an apartment myself in Harvard Square, on Bow Street. I guess that's about 10 minutes away.*

Applicant: *Oh, yeah, I know where that is.*

You: *Well, Mike, I wanted to get in touch with you because we've been looking at a lot of resumes, and yours stood out from the pack. I was wondering if I could ask you a couple of questions about your work experience.*

Applicant: *Great, go ahead.*

At this point, you'll want to pose some preliminary questions and *take written notes of the answers you receive.*

Remember: Your aim is to identify candidates who possess the requisite skills *and* demonstrate confidence, enthusiasm, experience, and dependability.

You should also feel free to ask for clarification of anything in the person's resume that confused you. For instance, if the person spent a particularly long time in a given position, you might ask what made him or her decide to stay there for so long…and why now is suddenly the time to leave.

Do not ask about the candidate's age, ethnic origin, marital status, religious beliefs, family status, social availability, sexual activities, or sexual orientation, either directly or indirectly. Posing questions like these is an excellent way to invite a lawsuit against your organization. Ask *only* questions that will help you determine the candidate's ability to effectively perform the duties you require. (See Chapter 13 for a more detailed discussion of illegal and ill-advised questions.)

During the call, listen for responses and stories that showcase the applicant's confidence, enthusiasm, experience, and dependability. Remember: People who like what they're doing tend to do a better job. This is not to say that everyone you interview must spout mindless good cheer at all times. But you do want to keep an ear out for applicants who sound engaged, intelligent, and motivated throughout the conversation. After all, that's how you want them to show up Monday morning!

Listen for indications that the person has already done some kind of research on your organization. This shows initiative and speaks well of the candidate's organizational skills. These days, it's so easy to conduct an online search that employers should probably be dubious of any applicant who *doesn't* attempt to research the company.

Steer clear of any candidate who focuses on negatives or appears eager to assign blame to colleagues, family members, or supervisors. As someone who has conducted a fair number of telephone interviews, I can assure you that it's surprisingly easy to determine from a single phone call or video chat if someone holds a basically cynical view of life.

Consider asking for the names of references you can call, and be suspicious if none you can actually speak to are forthcoming. I heard of an applicant who passed along to prospective employers an impressive list of references, all of whom happened to be out of the country and inaccessible for some months. It turned out (surprise, surprise) the candidate was camouflaging some serious deficiencies in his job history.

Be wary, too, of candidates who go out of their way to share carefully crafted malicious accounts of experiences with past employers or who volunteer information that is clearly confidential. The phrase "accident waiting to happen" should come to mind when you encounter them.

To maximize efficiency, you may want to prepare a "telephone or video interview form" that is specific to each position, using the job description you developed to identify required competencies and skills. I am presuming that you will have already eliminated candidates whose resumes lacked key education, experience, or other obvious requirements. Once you have established exactly those talents you are seeking, develop a short list of questions to home in on them. As you speak with each candidate, rate each answer on a scale of one to five. When you are finished with all your screening interviews, develop a simple matrix with the candidate's names down the left-hand side, the key competencies across the top, and pertinent scores in the resulting blocks. Simple addition will identify those candidates you should call for in-person interviews.

The telephone or video interview you conduct can be as long or as short as you feel appropriate. The main rule to follow is *not* to extend an offer for a face-to-face interview to an applicant whom you feel is not well-suited to the position or your company. If the screening interview has led you to this conclusion, there are two ways to wrap up. The first is probably the easiest. You simply say something like:

"Mike, I really appreciate your taking the time to talk about your background with me today. You've given me a lot to think about. You should know, though, that this is a very competitive position, and that we'll be talking to a lot of people over the next week or so. If we feel there's the possibility of a good match for this position or for any other opening, we will get back in touch with you at this number. Does that make sense?"

This allows you to exit the conversation gracefully, without deflating the person's ego too much—and without unnecessarily burning bridges. After all, if another position comes up for which this person *is* perfect, you *will* want to be able to get in touch.

There is another, more direct way to conclude a conversation with someone who does not meet your standards for the position:

"Mike, I've listened carefully to what you've told me today, and I have to be honest with you—I don't think we have a good match here. We're going to have to take a pass this time around."

Whichever approach you decide to use, bite the bullet and conclude the conversation *without* setting a time for a face-to-face interview with this person. It simply doesn't make sense for either of you to commit to a time-consuming, in-person meeting if you already suspect the candidate is under-qualified, hostile, uncommunicative, or in any way a bad choice for the position.

If, on the other hand, you decide after your initial screening interview that it makes sense to meet with this person, go ahead and set the date.

Regardless of whether the interview went well or poorly for the applicant, you should record your impressions of him or her right away. Write a few sentences summarizing your reactions to the applicant, as well as the reasons you decided to pursue further discussions—or not. The way you initially assess an applicant's performance can be a good signal of how the person will interact with you and others in the workplace.

In our litigious age, it's an unfortunate fact that you must protect yourself from disgruntled job seekers who file suits alleging illegal discrimination. That's why it's a good idea to record the legal and legitimate reasons for your rejection of a person's candidacy. Note any answers that left you cold. Briefly jot down the details of those elements of the person's background or work experience that seemed to represent a poor fit with the position.

On a less ominous note, you should specify in your notes how you felt about each of the people whom you *did* schedule for an interview. Was the chemistry between the two of you favorable? What memorable comments did the person make? What was the candidate's general level of knowledge about your industry and the likely day-to-day duties of the job? What made you decide to meet with this person? Was it the applicant's poise and unflappability? Her mastery of technical details? His knowledge of your company's products and services? The initiative she showed in asking you to meet with her personally?

I know a sales manager who never hires a salesperson unless he or she directly and clearly asks for an appointment or a job offer. He makes a habit of not calling candidates back after he interviews them. He's waiting for them to "ask for the order"…by asking for the job!

If you're not interviewing someone for a sales position, that's a fairly aggressive stance to take. I would, however, make note of all those applicants who take the bull by the horns and say something like, "I'm very excited about this opportunity and would like to start working for you" somewhere along the line. Such applicants should be given serious consideration; they are committed to making something good happen.

Your detailed notes will be invaluable later on in the process when you must consider each of the candidates individually before making a hiring decision. Of course, you also should take plenty of notes during your face-to-face interview, and, in the same way, summarize your reactions briefly at its conclusion.

3

Types of Interviews

An average interview should last 30 to 45 minutes, rarely more than an hour, except in the case of high-level executive positions. If you find yourself allotting an entire morning to a single interview, you might want to ask fewer than 101 questions...or talk a wee bit less about your own amazing career.

Although there is no rigid script you need to follow, most well-run interviews tend to follow a similar pattern:

- ◄ Introductions and small talk.

- ◄ An explanation of how the interview will be conducted and how it fits into the overall process.

- ◄ Interviewer questions.

- ◄ Interviewee questions.

- ◄ Where do we go from here?

Given the title of this book, you would think the third area would be the most important part of the interview. You would be wrong. *Every* step is an opportunity for you to test and gauge the applicant. For example, you may ask a seemingly innocent question like, "Did you have any trouble finding our office?" If the candidate claims her cross-town trip was comparable to Admiral Byrd's quest for the South Pole, you may set a record for the shortest interview! And if the first question she asks is about holidays and sick days, let her take an early vacation…today.

Some experts contend that many candidates are so well-prepared that most questions are useless—applicants have memorized answers to all of them. *All* of them? Please. A savvy interviewer may ask only one or two general questions, but dozens of probing, follow-up questions designed to glean the pertinent details of a candidate's experience, competencies, and skills…and uncover dishonesty, exaggeration, and hubris.

There are a number of styles and guiding philosophies when it comes to person-to-person interviews. The overall goal, of course, is to screen out applicants who lack the aptitudes (and attitudes) you're looking for, and to keep talking to only the most promising people.

Here's a summary of the methods and objectives of the most common approaches.

The behavioral interview

In this format, your conversation with the candidate will focus on his or her past experience and utilize a lot of probing questions. You're hoping to learn more about how he or she has already behaved in a variety of on-the-job situations. Then you'll attempt to use this information to extrapolate the person's future reactions on the job. Whatever your question, you should expect the answer to identify the **Problem** confronted, the **Action** taken, and the **Result** achieved. A good answer will also:

- ◄ Focus on the points important to you.
- ◄ Emphasize the most important points.
- ◄ Clearly not be memorized.
- ◄ Not introduce controversial subjects.

How did the person handle herself in some really tight spots? What kinds of on-the-job disasters has she survived? Did she do the right thing? What were the repercussions of the decisions she made?

You're not looking for perfection, but rather for a thorough understanding of what happened and why in a given workplace situation, and what was learned as a result. Beware of applicants who claim that they've never made mistakes or never found anything new to learn from a challenge. You're trying to ensure the candidate can actually "walk the walk," not just "talk the talk." You want to hear specific examples of problems he faced, the actions he took, and the results he achieved.

The competency-based interview

The competency-based interview is a highly popular evolution of the behavioral interview, based on the notion that any job requires candidates to be "competent" in specific areas. Author Paul Green defines a competency as "[a] written description of measurable work habits and personal skills used to achieve a work objective." Or, as author Robin Kessler defines them in her excellent book, *Competency-Based Interviews* (Career Press, 2006), competencies are "key characteristics it takes to be successful" in a particular job. So after identifying the competencies required for a job, an interviewer would then use behavior-based questions to gauge whether the candidate has them.

The following skills, in various combinations, could be considered key competencies for almost all jobs:

- ◄ Achievement orientation
- ◄ Accountability
- ◄ Adaptability
- ◄ Analytical thinking
- ◄ Conceptual thinking
- ◄ Conflict resolution
- ◄ Creative thinking
- ◄ Customer-service orientation
- ◄ Decision-making
- ◄ Independence
- ◄ Information-seeking
- ◄ Initiative
- ◄ Integrity
- ◄ Interpersonal skills
- ◄ Judgment
- ◄ Leadership
- ◄ Motivation
- ◄ Oral communication
- ◄ Planning and organizing
- ◄ Prioritizing and goal-setting
- ◄ Problem-solving
- ◄ Sociability

◄ Stress management

◄ Team-building

◄ Time management

◄ Written communication

Kessler claims, "At least half of the Fortune 500 and other major organizations in the U.S., in Europe, and internationally are now using competency-based systems to help select and manage their human resources."

The team interview

In many organizations, a team of three or more employees may interview an applicant for an open position, either separately or together. They may use similar or disparate styles.

The team interview can range from a pleasant conversation to a torturous interrogation. Typically, the applicant meets with a group of interviewers around a table in a conference room. A variation that's less stressful for the candidate involves a "tag team" approach, in which a single questioner exits and is followed by a different questioner a few minutes (or questions) later. (For the latter approach, it's essential to set up a coordinated strategy ahead of time, so as not to subject the applicant to the same questions four or five times in a row.)

The team members who take part in a group interview may be members of the department in which the candidate would work, or they may be a cross-section of employees from throughout the company. Whichever approach you take, there should be some format for a group discussion of the candidate's pros and cons *shortly after the interview takes place.* Ideally, you'll want to compare notes immediately after the group interview so as to record impressions while they're still fresh in everyone's mind.

As you discuss the results of a team interview, you'll want to consider each person's assessment of the candidate's suitability and experience. Ask about any instances that showed a candidate's lack of respect for the various members of the team. Did the candidate dismiss out of hand the concerns of an administrative or support an employee who was on the team? Was there a lack of respect for the organization's policies and procedures? Did the candidate treat every member of the team with respect and deference?

The team interview is a great way of minimizing the risk associated with the ever-more-expensive challenge of making the right hire. With more than one set of eyes and ears assessing the candidate, there's less chance you'll settle on the wrong person. Just be sure to canvas each member of the group and discuss all concerns openly and fully once the interview is complete. There's no point in going to the (sometimes significant) logistical trouble of scheduling a team interview if you're not going to elicit and record all of the feedback…or ignore it.

The case (situational) interview

"You're dealing with a publishing client. His printer just called and said the biggest book of the year had a typo on the spine. A bad typo. More than 100,000 books have already been printed. What should he do?"

If you are working at a consulting firm, law firm, or counseling organization, you probably are used to conducting this type of interview.

Responses to hypothetical questions can give you a greater understanding of someone's values, thinking processes, and practical experience. That's why situational interviewing has become so popular in recent years.

The premise is sound: Present the candidate with situations that might hypothetically occur on the job in order to gauge the degree to which he or she demonstrates the traits for success. It's hard for an interviewee to prepare ahead of time for these questions. That means you get to watch the person try to analyze an unfamiliar problem and develop a strategy to solve it, on the spot. Take notes on what happens after you ask a situational interview question; it's almost always interesting.

What you want to hear should ideally be a combination of real-world experience, inspired creativity, and the willingness to acknowledge when more information or assistance is in order. (Many interviewers pose hypothetical questions designed to smoke out people who find it impossible to reach out to other team members for help.) Does the person plunge right into the situation or take the time necessary to offer a reasoned, intelligent response to the question you've posed?

Situational interviews help you identify people who can step back, weigh the alternatives, and choose the best course of action. Just remember that technical skills are not all you're measuring. A highly skilled computer programmer, for instance, may constantly sow discord in the workplace or abuse rules concerning tardiness. You're interested in someone who not only *can* do the work, but also *will* do the work—and contribute as an effective, motivated member of the team.

(Although case interviews are geared to upper-echelon candidates, applicants for many different kinds of jobs may be given the opportunity to show what they can actually do on the job: Clerks may be given typing or filing tests; copy editors given minutes to edit a magazine article or book chapter; a salesperson may be asked to telephone and sell a prospect; or a computer programmer may be required to create some code.)

The stress interview

Formal qualifications are important, but in some jobs, the emotional demands, sudden emergencies, and breakneck pace of work can be downright intimidating—not once in a while, but every day. Even a candidate who knows all the technical moves may wilt under the glare of an etiquette-challenged boss or crumble when inheriting a surrealistically compressed deadline.

When you're hiring for such positions—whether you're looking for a commodities trader, air traffic controller, or prison guard—it may not be enough to ascertain that the candidate is capable of performing the job under the *best* conditions. You may well have to find out how the person will do under the very *worst* conditions. And that's where the stress interview comes in.

The stress interview is designed to cut through all the pleasantries and get right to the heart of the matter. A common question in this setting could sound gruff or rude—which is exactly how it's *supposed* to sound. Rather than a pleasant, "So, tell me about yourself," a stress interviewer may snarl (literally), "So, why the hell should I hire *you* for anything?"

Here are some techniques stress interviewers have been know to use:

◄ He ridicules everything the candidate says and questions why she's even interviewing at his company.

◄ He says nothing when the candidate enters the room…and for five minutes afterward…then just stares at the candidate after she answers his first question.

◄ He keeps the candidate waiting past the scheduled time and then keeps looking at his watch as she answers questions.

◄ He stares out the window and seems to be completely uninterested in everything the candidate has to say.

◄ He challenges every answer, disagrees with every opinion, and interrupts the candidate at every turn.

◄ He doesn't introduce himself when the candidate walks in, just hits her with a tough question.

◄ He takes phone calls, works on his computer, and/ or eats lunch as he interviews candidates.

◄ He may seat candidates in a broken chair, directly in front of a high-speed fan, or next to an open window... in the dead of winter.

The point of a stress interview is not to take pleasure in another human being's discomfort, but to find out exactly how the person would respond in a tough situation. Does the candidate maintain eye contact? Take a few seconds for a deep breath? Keep a level and professional tone of voice? Ask for more information? If so, you may have found someone who can take the heat.

But do yourself and the job seekers of the world a favor: Save the stress interview for candidates who really *are* being considered for extremely demanding positions. Otherwise, the kind of treatment cited above will just earn you and your company a reputation as an uninviting sweatshop.

(Don't confuse a stress interview with a *negative* interview, which is sometimes an effective technique. In the latter, the interviewer merely stresses the negative aspects of the job at every opportunity. He may even make some up: "Would you have any problem cleaning the toilets every Saturday morning?" or, "Will three hours of daily overtime be a problem for you?" It still may be an unpleasant interview for a candidate, but it isn't a sadistic one.

The brainteaser interview

As Microsoft interviewers have famously been known to ask, "How would you move Mt. Fuji?" The list of questions designed to assess how *creatively* an applicant approaches a problem—as opposed to the logical approach case interviews are designed to highlight—are virtually unlimited:

◄ How many oil wells are there in Texas?

◄ How many dentists are there in Poland?

◄ How many dollar bills (or pennies or dimes or quarters) would it take to fill up this room?

◄ How much did the people who attended last year's Super Bowl weigh?

Advocates of brainteaser interviews believe these types of questions are particularly useful when interviewing someone for either a highly creative position or one that requires superior analytical skills. Before you think of asking these types of questions, make sure the supposedly analytical or problem-solving skills they purport to elicit are key competencies for the position. Then you may want to ask yourself if how a person attempts to answer this type of question actually reflects how smart they are, how they think, or how they will approach on-the-job challenges.

Follow-up interviews

Though some strategies are more popular than others, many savvy interviewers consider all of the types of interviews you've just explored to be effective ways to get an understanding of what makes a candidate tick during an early face-to-face meeting. Once you bring someone back for the second interview, however, the stakes are considerably higher. An approach that at least includes, if not features, a team interview is highly recommended during this second level of interviewing.

Sadly, this advice is rarely implemented in today's workplace. A common (and often ill-fated) approach is for an experienced screener to handle the initial interview, and for the hiring manager to conduct the next discussion with the applicant in a one-on-one setting. The problem is that many managers lack formal or informal training in conducting interviews of any kind. As a result, quite a few are just as nervous as the job seekers they're interviewing. Is it really that surprising that, left to their own devices, they don't always make the best hiring decisions?

If you're a hiring manager who must evaluate a candidate during a hiring interview, my advice is three-fold:

1. Finish reading and re-reading this book from cover to cover.

2. Set up a *written* interview outline ahead of time. In other words, don't wing it. Decide what you want to learn about this applicant and which questions from this book's successive chapters will help you get the information you need.

3. Get other team members involved in the interview process and compare notes before you make a final decision.

One last piece of advice on the mechanics of the hiring interview: You'll no doubt be talking to multiple applicants, looking for that unique blend of confidence, enthusiasm, experience, and dependability that screams "hire me." It's quite common, however, to find yourself looking at two or more applicants who display such traits in abundance. All other factors being equal, you'll want to establish some kind of tie-breaker.

One of my favorite tie-breakers is to ask an applicant what books, courses, or seminars have helped him or her onto a path of personal self-improvement—and when. The more responsibility someone has demonstrated for his own personal growth, the more credit he gets. The more frequently a person tries to learn about how to be a happier, more productive, better-balanced person, the more I want that person on my team.

Now that you've got a sense of what the interview process feels like, how can you be sure you're effectively evaluating all the information you'll be receiving from all those enthusiastically motivated, top-tier candidates you've found?

That's what you'll find out about in the next chapter.

4

HERE WE GO

Effective interviewing requires both listening and observational skills. Tone of voice (including verbal timing) and body language play incredibly important roles in human interaction. In fact, it's been estimated that far more than half of what actually influences people is attributable to factors *other than* the *literal* content of the words they hear.

It follows, then, that the words a candidate uses during an interview are barely a corner of the picture he or she will paint for you. In this chapter, I'll give you powerful tools for interpreting the *non*verbal messages you receive from the job candidates you interview. I'll also cover some common occurrences—if a candidate is late, won't talk, or won't shut up—give you general guidelines for handling them, and discuss the "icebreaker" questions some candidates may consider "throwaways," but you shouldn't.

What to look for: the initial greeting

When you first encounter the candidate, silently ask yourself the following questions. The more often you can answer yes, the more likely it is that you've been blessed with a poised, confident candidate. Of course, no one is suggesting that confidence and social graces can compensate for lack of ability in the workplace. But in a perfect world, wouldn't you prefer to work with someone who meets all of the formal qualifications *and* has enough self-confidence to interact well with others?

- ◄ Did the candidate grip your hand firmly, avoiding both the "bone-crusher" and the "wet fish" approach?
- ◄ Did the candidate shake your hand with purpose?
- ◄ Did the candidate hold the shake for an appropriate period, neither too short nor too long?
- ◄ Did the candidate use one hand? (A two-handed handshake is often regarded as a sign of over-familiarity, though there are some regional/cultural exceptions to this rule.)
- ◄ Did the candidate look you in the eye?
- ◄ Did the candidate smile?
- ◄ Did the candidate use your name when greeting you?

What to look for: body language

Once the candidate takes a seat, you'll be doing the lion's share of the talking to begin the meeting. This is when the person is likely to be the most nervous, and when rapport-building questions will be most welcome. *After* you have put the person at ease by asking a few such questions, begin to monitor his or her gaze, physical posture, and general bearing. Use the following questions as a rough guideline, and take discreet notes as the interview moves forward. The more "yes" answers you record, the more comfortable (and, presumably, forthcoming) the person is likely to feel interacting with you.

◄ Does the candidate make appropriate intermittent eye contact with you—neither staring too long nor avoiding your gaze?

◄ Is eye contact broken only at natural points in the discussion, rather than suddenly, as in the middle of an exchange?

◄ Is the candidate's mouth relaxed? (A tightly clenched jaw, pursed lips, or a forced smile may indicate problems handling stress.)

◄ Is the candidate's forehead and eyebrow area relaxed?

◄ Does the candidate occasionally smile naturally?

◄ Does the person avoid nodding very rapidly for long periods of time while you're speaking? (This is shorthand for "Be quiet and let me say something now," and it is inappropriate in an interview setting.)

◄ Does the candidate move his or her hands so much or in such a weird manner that you actually notice? (Constant twitching of the fingers—or even worse, knuckle-cracking—may mean you're dealing with a person who simply can't calm down. Yes, an interview is an unsettling experience, but so are some of the tasks this person will have to perform on the job!)

◄ On a similar note, does the candidate avoid shuffling and tapping his or her feet?

◄ Is the candidate's posture good? (Slumping in one's chair may be sending a silent message: "I'm not even trying to make a good impression." If you hire him or her, you may encounter that attitude on a daily basis.)

◄ Are the candidate's eyes usually gazing forward, rather than darting all over the room?

◄ Is the candidate's head upright?

◄ Does the candidate tend to sit with crossed arms? (This may signal either a confrontational attitude or a sense of deep insecurity, neither of which is a positive sign.)

◄ Does the person appear to be breathing regularly and deeply?

◄ Is the person's personal hygiene and grooming acceptable? (Would you want to sit next to this person during a long meeting? Ask yourself: If the candidate won't make an effort to clean up his or her act for a job interview, what will an average workday be like?)

What to listen for: length, tone, and timing of responses

What the candidate says is certainly important, but so is *how* he or she says it. Make circumspect written notes if you cannot answer "yes" to all of the following questions during the interview. Three or more such negative notes during the course of the interview should raise questions about a candidate's social skills.

◄ Does the candidate respond in a clear, comprehensible, and confident tone of voice?

◄ Does the candidate avoid prolonged pauses in sentences?

◄ Is the candidate's speaking rhythm consistent and totally appropriate?

◄ Does the candidate avoid rambling answers?

◄ Does each of the candidate's answers have a clear concluding point, or do they all seem to just trail off into nothingness?

◄ Does the candidate avoid interrupting you? (Breaking in while a prospective employer is speaking shows poor judgment and underdeveloped people skills.)

◄ Does the candidate take the time to consider difficult questions before plunging in to answer them?

◄ Does the candidate ask for additional information or clarification when dealing with complex or incomplete questions?

◄ Does the candidate offer answers that are consistent with one another?

In *Competency-Based Interviews*, Robin Kessler asserts that candidates who are probably lying:

◄ Offer nonsensical or contradictory examples.

◄ Say one thing but reveal another through their body language.

◄ Are highly nervous and/or avoid eye contact.

◄ Move less than truthful candidates.

◄ Talk slower than other candidates.

◄ Often give one-word answers with no elaboration or examples.

◄ Pause before answering questions and often during answers.

◄ Tend to generalize and avoid citing specific examples.

◄ May guard their mouths, touch their noses, and rub their eyes.

Assuming that anyone who is nervous, pauses, or has allergies (rubbing one's eyes) is lying is obviously no way to treat interviewees, but the more such signs you observe, the more on your guard you should be.

As you monitor nonverbal signals during the interview, bear in mind that physical actions and vocal delivery should support the answers the interviewee provides. A candidate who assures you that he has what it takes to survive the ups and downs of a career in sales, but looks pale and shell-shocked when you mention that you're interviewing other candidates, is sending two very different messages. The "lyrics" may be saying "I can handle rejection," but the "music" should convince you otherwise.

What if the candidate shows up late?

A candidate who is even modestly prepared will usually make sure to arrive at your office 15 minutes early to get the lay of the land, freshen up, and calm down. Even if the unexpected pops up—traffic is snarled, a baby gets sick, the alarm malfunctions—a responsible candidate will do one of three things:

1. If he's on his way and will be slightly late, he will call.

2. If she's allowed enough extra time, she may calmly deal with an unexpected development and still arrive on time. If she's smart, you won't even know anything untoward occurred. (Why introduce a negative into the conversation?) A savvy candidate should have scouted your location beforehand and prepared alternate routes to avoid potential traffic problems.

3. If it's impossible to make the appointment at all, a good candidate will call you at least 15 minutes beforehand to explain what went wrong and attempt to reschedule. It's up to you how you respond to such a phone call. Accidents and emergencies happen and, as long as you are notified beforehand and not two hours after the fact, you may choose to give candidates the benefit of the doubt.

What if you never get a phone call and the candidate is significantly late? I would consider it a mark against him, especially if he fails to bring it up or sufficiently explain his reasons for the lateness. (Despite the usual advice to "avoid negatives" in an interview, this just begs for an explanation, and not offering one is a bigger negative.)

What if the candidate spouts generalities?

It's up to you to ask the probing questions necessary to translate some of a candidate's repetitive adjectives—"hard-working," "responsible," "loyal," "creative," and so on—into specific examples that demonstrate the experience and competencies you're seeking.

This may be due to simple nervousness or be evidence that there are very few specifics to cite. Keep probing: "I notice on your resume that you worked in the marketing department at Acme Co. for two years. What specific projects did you work on? What were your daily responsibilities? Whom did you report to?"

If necessary, you may have to clearly state that you require more than generalities to make a positive decision: "I appreciate your self-evaluation and I'm sure you are hard-working, intelligent, and so on, but I need you to cite and discuss some specific examples from your work experience that illustrate those traits."

If, despite your best efforts, you get little or nothing in return, you probably should assume that the candidate has added a bit of fluff to the resume and is having a hard time giving you specifics…because they just don't exist.

What if you catch the candidate in a bold-faced lie?

I doubt there's anyone out there who hasn't attempted to make a lowly, repetitive job sound a bit more glamorous and responsible than it really was. Or someone who "forgot" to put a short-term job on their resume and extended their stay at another by a month or two to cover it up. And you may decide to ignore such little white lies and continue the interview.

However, a truly blatant lie—claiming to have worked at a company when he didn't, altering a job title, vastly exaggerating duties and responsibilities, lying about her salary history, claiming a college degree that doesn't exist—is likely a clear reason to immediately end the interview.

What if the candidate is silent?

There are shy people, and there are those who become overly nervous during the interview process, no matter how gracious and friendly you are as an interviewer. What do you do when the person in front of you seems to be applying for the position of "clam"?

Thinking or acting impatiently will most likely exacerbate the situation, turning a nervous candidate into a potentially comatose one! Let him know that you appreciate that the artificial nature of an interview can make some people overly nervous. Encourage him to take a couple of deep breaths. Smile, relax, and urge *him* to relax. If nothing works, you may consider re-scheduling for another time.

What if the candidate talks very little?

There may be an occasion or two during the interview when you receive a brief, seemingly content-free answer along the lines of "I don't know" or "Sure, all the time" or "When there were problems, I sat down with people and worked them out." In such situations, you should ask a relevant probing question: "Can you give me a specific example that would show me what happened when you took that approach with a coworker?" "Can you further explain why you feel that project failed and what you could have done differently to influence the outcome?"

If the probing question results in yet another curt non-response, guess what? This person is not playing ball with you. Proceed with caution. The interviewee may be hiding something or have sub-par communication skills.

What if the candidate won't shut up?

You smile and say, "So, tell me a little about yourself," and before you know it, 10 minutes have elapsed and he's still discussing his middle school accomplishments. Perhaps he's just a talker, or maybe his verbal diarrhea is the way he responds to an attack of interview nerves. In either case, it's your job to handle his verbosity.

Make your questions as focused as possible to encourage equally focused responses. If the candidate still believes the journey to the end of the interview should explore every highway and byway along the road, attempt to insert a new question into any pause.

What if nothing you do blunts the verbal assault? I would ask myself whether such verbosity will harm the environment for others (to which the answer would probably be a resounding "yes"), then let him talk his way into some other company.

What if the candidate is obviously under- or overqualified?

If the candidate's experience, education, demeanor, and behavior clearly bear as much resemblance to the job as I do to Brad Pitt, you'll want to save the time and energy of continuing an interview that will clearly end up in a terse letter of rejection. Cut your losses early, and let the candidate know that the skills and experience she has simply don't match those of the job. Be polite, be nice, but be firm and move on to a more qualified interviewee. (Then ask yourself how she ever made it through the screening process.)

You should probably question the motivation of someone willing to "do almost anything." Will such an employee just show up and do what's asked but nothing more? What about someone willing to work "for almost nothing"? It may be a cliché, but you do usually get what you pay for. And that is exactly what "almost nothing" is worth.

Especially for lower-level positions, you may prefer hiring someone who will enjoy doing exactly what he or she was hired to do, rather than someone who considers it merely a stepping-stone to bigger and better positions. Some employees will undoubtedly feel their positions are threatened by new subordinates who seem more qualified than they.

On the other hand, an obviously overqualified candidate may present you with different options. He may be completely wrong for this job but perfect for another, unadvertised position in your area. He may be a great candidate for a job with another department or division. She may be a candidate to keep on file for a job opening that occurs in the future (presuming you're impressed by her demeanor, behavior, and attitude). Or, and this depends very much on your own circumstances, she may still be a candidate for this position because of her own situation. And, because of her obvious over-qualification, she may be far more valuable even in the short term than a more "perfect" long-term candidate. If an overqualified candidate is willing to make a commitment—six months minimally, perhaps a year—and take the high end of the salary offered but not more, you may be better off hiring her for the short term.

It's important to appreciate that a surprising percentage of both verbal and nonverbal behavior is culturally based; what Americans consider "getting right down to business," for example, Japanese consider downright rude. So if you are conducting interviews in a country other than the United States, I urge you to consult an international etiquette guide such as Ann Marie Sabath's *Business Etiquette*, which will help you adapt these questions for each particular country.

There are no unimportant questions

Some questions are viewed by a segment of candidates as "throwaways," the answers to which are, for the most part, unimportant.

I don't believe in "throwaways," and I think every answer tells a story or reveals another aspect of a candidate's personality or thinking processes. You should be assessing them from the moment they walk in the door (or answer the phone) to the moment you offer them the job (or escort them out of the building).

Many interviewers use these questions as "icebreakers," believing that they give a false, informal impression of "let's just chat, shall we?" and lead candidates to drop their interview guard. Some interviewees, dismissed after only a few minutes, belatedly discover that these innocent questions "ice-picked" their chance for the job.

Other questions, primarily those regarding an applicant's health, willingness to travel or relocate, or availability, may be so important to the job at hand that they are near the top of the list of the questions you ask during the first five minutes of every interview. The more important relocation or travel is, for example, the earlier I would ask those questions in the interview (because a negative answer may end the interview then and there).

As the head of recruiting for a rather large company, a friend of mine spent weeks at a time interviewing scores of candidates for a wide variety of openings. With so much practice, she became very good at identifying unsuitable candidates in minutes—and "releasing" the unsuspecting person with a simple, "Thanks for stopping by" before the interview even got underway!

Here's how it worked: On greeting a young applicant for a field sales position, my friend asked, "How are you?" The applicant immediately began whining that it was raining and she had a run in her stocking.

My friend turned to her and, feigning embarrassment, said, "Oh! Are you here to apply for that field sales position? I'm sorry. We forgot to call. We filled the position yesterday. But we'll keep you in mind for similar positions. Thanks for stopping by."

Q: *How are you today?*

What do you want to hear?

She is doing just fine, thank you. No trouble finding your offices, because, of course, she took the time to get directions from your assistant.

You should expect a positive answer to virtually any question, no matter how off-hand it seems to the candidate. Nothing negative (even the crummy weather!) should affect his or her responses.

Since my recruiter friend told me her little story, I know I pay much more attention to the answers candidates give to these little "throwaway" questions.

Variations

◄ Did you have any trouble finding us?

◄ Where are you staying? Do you like the hotel?

◄ How was your flight?

Q: *Who are your heroes and why?*

What do you want to hear?

Candidates playing it safe may settle on "Mother Theresa," "Thomas Jefferson," or a parent, fully prepared to enlighten you in boring detail. But not all candidates will take the opportunity to avoid controversy. You may learn more than they want you to know if they cite Rush Limbaugh, Rachel Maddow, a bizarre fantasy figure, or vapid celebrity. Ask yourself what such choices should tell you about: a) their political persuasion; b) their TV- and movie-watching habits; or c) their subscriptions to *US Weekly* and *Star*. Then act accordingly.

Q: *What was the last book you read?*

What do you want to hear?

You should ask this question if you believe that what someone chooses to read speaks volumes about what kind of a person he is.

Of course, savvy candidates know that, right or wrong, many interviewers seem to think that people who read nonfiction are more interested in the world about them than fiction readers, who are just looking for escape. So rather than talking about the latest thriller they couldn't put down, they will instead quote a popular how-to book they may actually have read (but certainly may not have). Thus you will be told that they're interested in *The Seven Habits of Highly Successful People* or *The Discipline of Market Leaders*, and never admit to knowing Grisham or King or Cornwall.

The more well-read and widely read you are, the more you may choose to make what seemed a simple "throwaway" question into a more detailed conversation about literature, culture, and art. It may have little or nothing to do with your business or the job at hand, but it certainly will give you a better handle on the person sitting before you.

 Thumbs down

◄ Anyone who asks, "What's a book?"

◄ Anyone who can't remember or admits having read a book—somewhere back in the fourth grade or so.

Is there really a job where reading is not somehow involved? And if there were, wouldn't you still want someone who reads an occasional book, if only a thriller or trashy romance novel? Well, if only a thriller?

Variations

◄   Why did you choose that book?

◄   How many books do you read in a month, a year?

◄   What's your favorite book?

◄   Who's your favorite author?

◄   Who's your favorite novelist?

◄   What magazines do you read regularly?

◄   Where do you get your news?

Q: *What was the last movie you saw?*

What do you want to hear?

Probably not a dissertation about her preference for foreign films or left-wing documentaries or a rhapsody about his collection of *Scream* movies. Again, who is this person outside of work? What does he or she really like to do? Any glimpse will simply give you one more brush stroke to add to their portraits.

An experienced interviewee will not allow such "conversational" questions to lull him into a false sense of security. He will remember that this is still a job interview, not a meeting of the local literary society or movie fan club. So he will undoubtedly cite a movie he thinks you'll approve of rather than one that accurately reflects his literary or cinematic tastes. But not everyone is experienced, and you may get that extra personal glimpse you're seeking.

Variations

◄ What three people would you most like to have dinner with?

◄ What other person would you invite to a desert island?

◄ Who's your favorite actor?

◄ What's your favorite movie?

◄ What's your favorite TV show?

Q: If I went on to your Facebook page right now, what would I find?

What do you want to hear?

We have all been warned that anything posted online never dies, yet you may find candidates who have posted pictures with drink in hand (or face on floor). What were they thinking? Not much.

You may not be intimately involved with social media yourself, but your company may be one of the many that now routinely check applicants' Facebook pages, Twitter feeds, blogs, and other social media sites. Candidates should be prepared for questions about their Internet presence that they wouldn't have faced just a few years ago.

Variations

◄ How many friends do you have on Facebook?

◄ How many Twitter followers do you have?

◄ Who do you follow on Twitter?

◄ What's your favorite website?

◄ What's your favorite podcast?

◄ What's your favorite blog?

◄   What's the most-used app on your phone?

◄   How much time do you spend on social media?

Q: *What do you like to do when you're not at work?*

What do you want to hear?

Many employers subscribe to the theory "If you want something done, give it to a busy person." If you agree, then you will look kindly on a candidate who assures you she is an active, vital, well-rounded individual. You may not get a lot of information from this question; a smart candidate will do everything in his power to remain uncontroversial, citing "reading" and "tennis," for example, rather than "skydiving" and "picketing furriers."

  Thumbs up

An individual whose outside interests (or, at least, those being revealed to you) bear some relationship to her career. For example, if you're seeking someone for a position as a bookstore manager, you will react positively to a candidate who reads three books a week, negatively to one who reveals an addiction to helicopter skiing.

Activities that show that the candidate is community-minded and people-oriented—the chamber of commerce, Toastmasters, the Rotary Club, or fund-raising for charities.

There should be no problem with a candidate demonstrating an interest in various sports activities—participating in team sports, coaching children, or indulging in activities such as swimming, running, walking, or bicycling. It shows he or she is particularly health-conscious, involved, and physically active.

Thumbs down

Couch potatoes: "I'm a Giants fan. I never miss a game. I also catch every rerun of my 17 favorite shows."

Those who are so active they are heading for a collapse: "I play racquetball, coach a softball team, am on the board of directors of the local museum, plan to run for city council this fall and, in my spare time, attend lectures on "Egyptology." (Whew! Where will she find the time to actually work?)

Those who boast about dangerous activities: "I like to challenge myself. Next week, I'm signed up for another hang-gliding trip. I need something to keep me pumped up until rugby season starts." It wouldn't take much to envision a prolonged sick leave on the horizon, a fact that might disqualify an otherwise-viable candidate.

A candidate who isn't smart enough to avoid sensitive or controversial topics, especially politics and religion: "I'm always on the front lines at PETA demonstrations." Or "I give all my money to the Crusade to Convert the World to (fill in the blank) religion."

Variations

◄ What are your hobbies?

◄ What are your favorite activities in your off hours?

◄ What did you do last weekend?

◄ Where did you go on your last vacation?

◄ What do you spend your extra money on?

Q: Are you in good health? What do you do to stay in shape?

What do you want to hear?

You and your company probably have more than a passing interest in your employees' health. Most companies are looking for ways to keep the overall cost of health insurance from skyrocketing, and most managers want to know that a new hire won't be felled by every flu bug that makes the rounds—and on sick leave when they need her most. In fact, many employers make job offers contingent on a candidate's passing a physical examination.

You shouldn't expect (or necessarily want) an exercise nut or someone ready to participate in a triathlon, but probably want to hear that a candidate regularly participates in an activity that provides at least some health benefit, such as yard work, home repairs, or even walking the dog.

There are two more specific questions that, if relevant, should probably be asked very early in the process. The answer to either could well end the interview.

Q: Are you willing to travel?

What do you want to hear?

"Yes, of course. My family understands the demands of my career and is supportive when I need to spend some time away from home. Approximately how many days per month would I be required to be on the road?"

Although not too many people relish being on the road three weeks out of four, such a schedule is inherent in some jobs and whoever is interviewing for them should certainly be prepared for those travel requirements.

Again, the more travel that is inherent to the job you have open, the more likely I would ask this question *early* in the process. Unless you have a good screening process, you may well get the occasional applicant who considers one day a month "excessive travel"—and you need a rep out of the office four days a week.

Q: *Are you willing to relocate?*

What do you want to hear?

I presume you're only asking this question if relocation is a clear and immediate necessity (or, at the very least, a real possibility within a year or two). If you revealed this fact in an ad or post for the position, you should expect a pretty enthusiastic response—"Absolutely. In fact, I would look forward to the chance to live elsewhere and experience a different lifestyle and meet new people"—unless yet another applicant has decided that "requirements" you've noted somehow don't apply to him or her.

If you've surprised someone with the news, you should expect a more restrained (but still relatively positive) reply:

"Well, not unless the job is so terrific that it would be worth uprooting my family and leaving my relatives and friends. Does this position require a move? I'm obviously very interested in it, so I might consider relocating."

Variation

◄   Do you have any location preferences?

5

TELL ME A LITTLE
ABOUT YOURSELF

Richard thinks he's a pretty good interviewer. He has a list of 15 questions he asks every candidate—same questions, same order, every time. He takes notes on their answers, even asks an occasional follow-up question. He's friendly, humorous, and excited about working at Netcorp.com. As he tells the candidate...in detail...for *hours*. Then he wonders why only a small fraction of his hires pan out.

The purpose of the interview is to get the *candidate* talking, and talking, and talking. I'm sincerely happy you like your job, admire your boss, and love your company. But don't let this adoration lead to an interview in which you talk three times more than the interviewee!

I've never really understood the interviewer who thinks telling the story of his life is pertinent. Why do some interviewers do it? Part nervousness, part inexperience, but mostly because they have the mistaken notion they have to sell the interviewee on the company, rather than the other way around. There *are* instances and reasons why this *may* be necessary: periods of low unemployment, a glut of particular jobs and a dearth of qualified candidates, or a candidate who's so desirable you know you have to outsell and outbid your competition for his or her services. But don't make it a rule to turn the interview into a sales conference. Under most circumstances, let the candidate do the talking—and the selling—and sit back and decide if you're ready to buy.

What's ideal? I doubt there's a definitive answer or one based on any systematic study, so I'll just lay out my own opinion: If you interview someone for an hour and spend more than 15 minutes talking yourself, you're letting *them* interview *you*.

The more you find yourself blathering on about the wonderfulness of everything from the cafeteria to your newly acquired file cabinet, the less likely you are to ask the open-ended, probing questions you need to identify the right person for the job.

So make it a habit to ask beautifully broad, open-ended questions at the start of every interview. Get them talking, and keep your own tongue on a leash.

Q: *Tell me a little about yourself.*

This question is your icebreaker. It gives you a chance to gauge initial chemistry, get a little insight into the cipher sitting before you, and makes *him* do all the talking for at least a couple of minutes!

Should this time-tested question catch her unprepared? Certainly not. Every interview book I've ever seen (or written) has pretty much guaranteed that this will be one of the first three questions asked, often the very first one!

What if she hems and haws her way through a disjointed, free-associating discourse that starts in kindergarten class and, 10 minutes later, is just getting into the details of those eighth-grade soccer tryouts? You just tied the record for the shortest interview of the week. Thank her and move on to the next candidate.

What do you want to hear?

It's just a starting point, but you want a well-thought-out, logically sequenced summary of the candidate's experience, skills, talents, and schooling. A plus is if this tightly focused introduction (of about 250 to 350 words) clearly and succinctly connects the candidate's experience to the requirements of the position. So a smart interviewee should have prepared an "opening statement" that consists of:

- ◄ A brief introduction.

- ◄ Key accomplishments.

- ◄ Key strengths demonstrated by these accomplishments.

- ◄ The importance of these strengths and accomplishments to you, the prospective employer.

- ◄ Where and how the candidate sees himself developing in the position for which he is applying (tempered with the right amount of self-deprecating humor and modesty).

 Thumbs up

So many books (including mine) have touted proper preparation for "Tell me about yourself" that it's probably the most rehearsed answer you'll get. If you're lucky, you'll hear something like what Barb, a college graduate applying for an entry-level sales position, said:

"I've always been able to get along with different types of people. I think it's because I'm a good talker and an even better listener. (Modestly introduces herself, while immediately laying claim to the most important skills a good salesperson should have.)

"During my senior year in high school, when I began thinking seriously about which careers I'd be best suited for, sales came to mind almost immediately. In high school and during my summer breaks from college, I worked various part-time jobs at retail outlets. (Demonstrates industriousness and at least some related experience.) *Unlike most of my friends, I actually liked dealing with the public.* (Conveys enthusiasm for selling.)

"However, I also realized that retail had its limitations, so I went on to read about other types of sales positions. I was particularly fascinated by what is usually described as consultative selling. I like the idea of going to a client you have really done your homework on and showing him how your products can help him solve one of his nagging problems, and then following through on that. (Shows interest and enthusiasm for the job.)

"After I wrote a term paper on consultative selling in my senior year of college, I started looking for companies at which I could learn and refine the skills shared by people who are working as account executives. (Shows initiative both in researching the area of consultative selling to write a term paper and then researching prospective companies.)

"That led me to your company, Mr. Sheldon. I find the prospect of working with companies to increase the energy efficiency of their installations exciting. I've also learned some things about your sales training programs. They sound like they're on the cutting edge. (Gives evidence that she is an enthusiastic self-starter.)

"I guess the only thing I find a little daunting about the prospect of working at Co-generation, Inc., is selling that highly technical equipment without a degree in engineering. By the way, what sort of support does your technical staff lend to the sales effort?" (Demonstrates that she is willing to learn what she doesn't know and closes by deferring to the interviewer's authority. By asking a question the interviewer must answer, Barb has also given herself a little breather. Now the conversational ball sits squarely in your court.)

Based on the apparent sincerity and detail of her answers, it's not a bad little "speech" of only 250 words, is it?

With nearly a decade of experience in his field, Ken is applying for a job as a district general manager for a firm that provides maintenance services to commercial and residential properties.

Going into the interview, he knows he has a couple of strikes against him. First of all, he's already held four jobs, so he's moved around a bit. And he doesn't yet have the management experience required by the job—virtually the equivalent of running a business with revenues of $12 million a year.

But because he has anticipated what might otherwise have been a devastating first interview question—"Tell me something that will help me get a better feel for you than what I get here on the resume" (a nice variation on "Tell me about yourself")—Ken is prepared with this winning counter-punch:

"I'm a hard worker who loves this business. I've been an asset to the employers I've had, and my experience would make me an even greater asset to you.

"I think these are the most exciting times that I've ever seen in this business. Sure, there's so much more competition now, and it's harder than ever to get really good help. But all the indications are

that more and more companies will outsource their maintenance needs and that more two-income households will require the services that we provide.

"How do we get a bigger share of this business? How do we recruit and train the best personnel? Because they are, after all, key to our success. Those are the main challenges managers face in this industry.

"I can help your company meet those challenges. While resumes don't tell the whole story, mine demonstrates that I'm a hard worker. I've had promotions at every company I've worked for.

"I would bring a unique perspective to the position because I've been a doer, as well as a supervisor. The people who have worked for me have always respected my judgment, because they know I have a very good understanding of what they do.

"And I have solid business sense. I'm great at controlling expenses. I deploy staff efficiently. I'm fair. And I have a knack for getting along with customers.

"I've always admired your company. I must admit I have adopted some of CleanShine's methods and applied them in the companies I've worked for.

"I see now that you're branching into lawn care. I worked for a landscaping business during my high school summers. How is that business going?"

In a mere 275 words, Ken managed to:

◄ *Focus you only on the positive aspects of his resume.* Sure, he has changed jobs, but after this answer, you're likely to think, "Gee, look at all he's managed to accomplish everywhere he's been."

◄ *Get the interview started in the direction he wanted it to go.* He demonstrated leadership abilities, experience, and a good understanding of the market.

◄ *Introduce just the right amount of humility.* While taking every opportunity to turn the spotlight on his many accomplishments and professional strengths, Ken portrayed himself as a roll-up-the-sleeves type of manager who will be equally at ease with both blue-collar workers and the "suits" back at headquarters.

◄ *Turn the interview back over to you by asking a very informed question.*

Although both Ken and Barb rehearsed their speeches, neither memorized them word-for-word. Ken additionally sprinkled in a little industry jargon here and there, which was entirely appropriate.

 Thumbs down

◄ *Lack of eye contact.* You're asking this question to get a little chemistry, and so far the candidate hasn't conjured up a reaction.

◄ *Lack of strong, positive phrases and words.* It may be your first question and, therefore, the first chance for the candidate to get off on the right foot. Shouldn't you be expecting words that convey enthusiasm, responsibility, dedication, and success? If the very first answer is uninspired (especially an answer we all assume has been prepared and even rehearsed), I have almost never seen the interview improve very much. Cut your losses and move on.

◄ *Lack of professional language appropriate to your industry, profession, or specialty.* This should be your tip-off that the candidate extolling her extensive experience is, at best, stretching the facts. I would expect even a neophyte to have done enough research to sound like she knows something of your world. Wouldn't you expect more from a supposed professional?

◄ *A general, meandering response that fails to cite specific accomplishments.* It's a plus if the candidate has been savvy enough to "edit" what we all know is a well-rehearsed set speech to ensure that it's relevant to the job at hand. Shouldn't you consider it a minus if all you've heard is a bunch of generalities with few or no examples to back them up?

◄ *No relevance to the job or your company.* Some candidates believe this question is an invitation to tell you about their hobbies, pets, favorite ice-cream flavor, or boy band. You may give them the initial benefit of the doubt, but I'd probe quickly for some job-related specifics.

◄ *Lack of enthusiasm.* If they aren't excited about interviewing for the job, why do you think they'll suddenly become so when you hire them?

◄ *Nervousness.* Some people are naturally nervous in the artificial and intimidating atmosphere of an interview, so I wouldn't consider this an automatic reason to have your assistant buzz you about that "emergency conference." But it could be a harbinger that something is lurking—a firing, a sexual harassment suit, *some*thing that isn't going to make your day. Try to make the atmosphere less formal than usual: smile, put them at ease, and then see what develops.

◄ *Even if they have solid experience, their skills don't match your needs.* I'm always amazed at how many interviewers believe that an interview must last a certain amount of time (20 minutes, half an hour, an hour) when it's apparent *in the first three minutes* that the candidate is overqualified, under-qualified, or "misqualified" for the job they're trying to fill. There is nothing wrong with continuing the interview to ascertain whether he or she is a good candidate for another (even future) opening. But don't kid yourself—this candidate is not right for *you now.*

◄ *Someone who asks a clarifying question,* such as "What exactly do you want to know?" or "Which particular areas would you like me to talk about?" As I said earlier, I find it hard to believe anyone interviewing for anything has not anticipated that this question will be asked. What does he *think* you want to know? His opinion about the latest celebrity gossip? You want to know about his experience, skills, talents, and education, and if he can't figure that out, you shouldn't go any further.

Variations

◄ What makes you special (unique, different)?

◄ What five adjectives describe you best?

◄ Rate yourself on a scale of 1 to 10.

◄ How would you describe your character?

◄ How would you describe your personality?

◄ Tell me something you really don't want me to know.

Despite the nuances, I wouldn't be surprised if a savvy candidate merely edited his or her "set piece" to respond to each of the above questions in essentially the same way. So although some of the questions appear to be more targeted, all six are really looking for the same information:

◄ Why are you here?

◄ Why should I hire you?

◄ Why should I consider you a strong candidate for this position?

◄ What's better about you than the other candidates I'm interviewing?

◄ What can you do for me that someone else can't?

These are more aggressive questions. While you should be expecting the same information, the tone of each of these questions is a bit more forceful: You're clearly attempting to make candidates fully aware that they're on the hot seat. This may be a matter of your own style, the introduction to your own brand of stress interview, or just a way to save time by seeing how they respond to pressure.

In one respect, I think phrasing your first question this way *helps* the candidate: You've virtually required that her answer match specific strengths, accomplishments, skills, and so on to job requirements you've already enumerated (in an ad or post, through human resources, wherever). You've given her a bit more direction than a simple question like "Tell me about yourself" would.

On the other hand, you've immediately given yourself an opportunity to measure the extent (or actual existence) of the pre-interview research the applicant has undertaken and the ability to separate the "misqualified" after a single question.

An applicant, for example, may emphasize her ability to meet deadlines and cite specific instances, which clearly shows she worked mostly by herself.

In the position you have available, the successful candidate may have to coddle and cajole a wide variety of managers in several offices across the country to get input for reports, then get each of them to sign off on the finished product. Although "tenacity" and "meeting deadlines" may have fallen trippingly off her tongue, you need a highly diplomatic team player, not a loner.

Q: *What are your strengths as an employee?*

What do you want to hear?

This is probably helpful to those who haven't prepared as well, as you're giving them the hint you want to ensure their experience, competencies, and skills match your needs and don't care about their captaincy of the chess club in junior high. Although it's still an open-ended question, it tends to focus the conversation too early. I prefer not to ask it, certainly not at the very beginning of an interview. The natural follow-up question, and the one some candidates may not be as prepared for, is "Go ahead and tell me about your biggest weaknesses." Either question may help you identify gaps in their qualifications.

Q: *How would your (best friend, favorite professor, mother, sibling, and so on) describe you?*

What do you want to hear?

Personally, I would start with the "best friend" variation if you're going to use this question. Supposedly, that's who should know the candidate best, so if you get a half-baked picture of the applicant, you'll know you can shorten the interview—by about seven-eighths of an hour. Another approach is to ask the applicant to describe his or her best friend and how they differ from each another. Because the candidate is supposedly describing her best friend, not herself, she may offer character insights you wouldn't get otherwise.

All of the other variations on this question can be used to home in on specific times (college, high school, last job) or just to get a fuller picture of the person. What someone's mother or father would say, for example, will often give you a clear illustration of the kind of environment in which the applicant was raised.

Variation

◄ How would someone who doesn't like you describe you?

A nefarious way to directly introduce a negative into the conversation, this question may reveal some flaws a candidate hoped to hide.

Q: *What do you want to be doing five years from now?*

What do you want to hear?

Are the candidate's goals and yours compatible? Is he looking for fast or steady growth in a position you know is a virtual dead end? Is she anticipating more money than you can ever pay? How have the candidate's goals and motivations changed as he has matured and gained work experience? If he has recently become a manager, how has that change affected his future career outlook? If she has realized she needs to acquire or hone a particular skill, how and when is she planning to do so?

This question is not as popular as it once was, because the pace of change at many corporations continues to accelerate.

You are probably more concerned about the candidate's ability to make a more immediate impact, so you may ask something like, "What will you be able to accomplish during your first ninety (100, 180) days on the job?"

 Thumbs up

Here's a good general answer, if only because it opens up so many specific areas for follow-up questions:

"That will ultimately depend on my performance on the job and on the growth and opportunities offered by my employer.

"I've already demonstrated leadership characteristics in all of the jobs I've held, so I'm very confident that I will take on progressively greater management responsibilities in the future. That suits me fine. I enjoy building a team, developing its goals, then working to accomplish them."

In other words, she wants "more"—more responsibility, more people reporting to her, more turf, even more money. A general answer (as above) is only a starting point; don't fail to ask the obvious follow-up questions (using the answer to the previous question as a guide):

◄ "Tell me about the last team you led."

◄ "Tell me about the last project your team undertook."

◄ "What was the most satisfying position you've held, and why?"

◄ "If I told you our growth was phenomenal and you could go as far as your abilities would take you, where would that be, and how quickly?"

Thumbs down

Anyone answering "Your job." It's a cliché.

Anyone who offers a "general" answer—that is, no specific goals, no matter how much you probe. That should be a tip-off that this particular candidate has not taken the time to really think about his future, which makes it impossible for *you* to assess whether there's a "fit" between his goals and yours.

Anyone who says she wants to be in the same job for which she's applying—unless it *is* a dead-end job and you'd be happy as punch if someone actually stayed longer than three weeks, unlike the last 14 people to hold the position.

Anyone whose answer reveals unrealistic expectations. A candidate should have some idea of the time it takes to climb the career ladder in your particular industry or company. Whereas someone hoping to go from account manager to CEO in two years should raise an obvious red flag, any expectations that are far too ambitious should give you pause. If a law school grad, for example, seeks to make partner in four years—when the average for all firms is seven and, for yours, 10—shouldn't that make you question the extent of her pre-interview research?

There's nothing wrong with being ambitious and confident, but a savvy interviewee should temper such boundless expectations during the interview. We all know that some candidates do successfully "break the rules," but most interviewers get a little nervous around people with unbridled ambition.

If you're worried that your company wouldn't be able to deliver on the promises a candidate wants to hear, you can ask a follow-up question: "How soon after you're hired do you think you can contribute to our success?" Even someone with a tremendous amount of pertinent experience knows full well that each company has its own particular ways of doing things and that the learning curve may be days, weeks, or months, depending on circumstances. So any candidate—but especially an overly ambitious young person—who blithely assures you she'll be productive from Day One is cause for concern. You're really trying to assess, in the case of an inexperienced person, how "trainable" she is, and she's just told you she thinks she already knows it all! Not a good start.

For some reason, some applicants fail to remember that this is an interview, not a conversation in a bar or with friends. As a result, you may also get some remarkable responses that can only be called "fantasies"—to be retired, own his own business, run an office in Paris—though why they would think any such answer is pertinent to their job search is beyond me.

Variations

◄ What are your most important long-term goals?

◄ Have you recently established any new objectives or goals?

◄ What do you want to do with your life?

◄ What do you want to be when you grow up?

Q: If you could change one thing about your personality, what would it be and why?

What do you want to hear?

A smart candidate will take a trait previously (or now) identified as a weakness and put together a brief answer that indicates awareness and motivation:

"I had a hard time with procrastination in college. But I licked it because burning the midnight oil all through exam week every semester was driving me nuts.

"I have to confess, I still have the urge to procrastinate. (He or she might smile disingenuously here.) *I wish that I never felt like putting things off, because I know what will happen if I do."*

 Thumbs down

A candidate who identifies a weakness that is job-related or, worse, essential to the job at hand (for example, an inability to work with others when the job on offer is highly team-based).

Anyone who identifies a weakness that is so basic or stupid that you have to wonder if that's the *biggest* thing they would try to change.

Beware of the unbelievable answer that is an attempt to skate by the question: "You know, I just work too hard. I have to take more time off than just Sunday from 5 a.m. to 7 a.m." Sure you do.

Variations

- ◄ Tell me about one thing in your life you're proudest of.

- ◄ Tell me about the worst decision you ever made.

- ◄ Tell me about the thing in your life you're most ashamed of.

- ◄ What's your greatest weakness?

The first question puts the candidate on preferable turf— a positive question one can answer positively. The latter three force one to turn negative questions into positive answers, and, because any negative question invites the unwary to descend into a sea of recriminations—"Working for that last jerk, let me tell you!"—they are a better test from your standpoint.

In all cases, you're inviting conversation but not as one-way or open-ended as earlier questions. These might well be follow-up questions if "Tell me about yourself" or something similar didn't reveal as much about the candidate as you hoped it would.

Q: *If you had all the time in the world and a bank account full of money, what would you do?*

What do you want to hear?

If we truly believed honesty was the best policy, I suspect many of us might actually blurt out, "Well, after I bought my houses, a yacht, and a plane, I would…" or some other fantastical plan. Some candidates will think this is a trick question, assuming you want them to humbly admit that despite their newfound fortune, they would still want to be a cog in your corporate machine. Perhaps there *are* a couple of people who could say that with a straight face…and even mean it. But I would wonder about their sanity.

Although this question clearly has nothing to do with the job for which you are interviewing this candidate, his response can give you a much greater understanding of how he thinks, his values, his aspirations, and his good sense. Listening to his answer, you should ask yourself:

◄ *Did the candidate pause and think before answering?* This is not a question most candidates would anticipate and, therefore, not one for which they will have a ready reply. The "trickier" they believe this question to be, the more time they should take to carefully frame their answer. Like a brainteaser interview, it's not like there is a list of "right" answers somewhere, so the candidate should immediately understand his thought process is more important than his words.

◄ *Was her answer consistent with the impression she has been trying to impart?* If she has taken pains to stress her empathy and charitable urges but gets mired in the details of her yacht's furnishings, you may begin to question the extent of her altruism. Shouldn't she be talking about the nonprofit foundation she intends to fund with her windfall?

In a similar vein, shouldn't a candidate who has tiresomely stressed his independence and entrepreneurial spirit start describing the various businesses he would consider starting?

◄ *Are his materialistic fantasies over the top?* Despite someone's declared plans to start a business, establish a foundation, or help out desperate relatives, it would be unusual if they completely ignored the very human urge to buy a few nice things. But if their new house would rival the Taj Mahal and they are thinking of buying an auto *company,* you may have received a realistic assessment of their view of money. If you are interviewing someone for a sales position, you will *want* her to be highly money-motivated. Otherwise, you may not want to subject yourself to someone who will ask for a raise within days of her hiring.

 Thumbs up

"When I went to college, I needed to work nearly 20 hours a week to help pay my tuition. I worked every summer from the time I was 14. And my career over the last decade has demonstrated my initiative, motivation, and work ethic. I am making more right now than either of my parents ever thought of earning, and I value being compensated for a job well done, but money has never been my primary motivation.

"So I don't think sudden wealth would radically change my lifestyle or my values, although a bigger apartment would definitely be on my list. More important would be using that money to create value in the world. I don't know what kind of enterprise I would create, but I suspect I would wind up working at it as much or more than I do now.

"If you'd like to make a sizeable donation to my bank account right now, I could give you a more detailed plan in a week!"

Although the candidate has welcomed his newfound wealth, he has not allowed himself to be overcome with fantasies *or forgotten he is in an interview*. His answer strongly asserts his self-identity as a hard worker at both the start and end of his answer. And although it is clear he will do something with all this cash, he acknowledges that it is a situation he has not thought about and doesn't attempt to provide details on a moment's notice.

Variations

◄ What would you do if you won the lottery tomorrow?

◄ If you were independently wealthy, would you be sitting here now?

◄ If I offered you a million dollars to start a business, what would it be?

Q: *What does "success" mean to you?*

What do you want to hear?

A good candidate should offer a balanced answer to this question, citing personal as well as professional examples. If his successes are exclusively job-related, you may wonder if he is little more than an automaton. However, if she goes on and on about her personal goals, you may get the impression she's uncommitted to working toward success on the job.

 Thumbs up

"I have always enjoyed supervising a design team. I've discovered that I'm better at working with other designers than designing everything myself. Unlike a lot of the people in my field, I'm able to relate to the requirements of the manufacturing department.

"So, I guess I'd say success means working with others to come up with efficient designs that can be up on the assembly line quickly. Of course, the financial rewards of managing a department give me the means to travel during my vacations. That's the thing I love most in my personal life."

 Thumbs down

◄ Incompatibility of his goals and yours.

◄ Lack of focus in her answer.

◄ Too general an answer, with no examples of what successes have already been achieved.

◄ Too many personal examples.

◄ Too many job-oriented examples.

Variations

◄ What does "achievement" mean to you?

◄ What does "challenge" mean to you?

◄ What does "problem" mean to you?

◄ What does "impossible" mean to you?

◄ What does "growth" mean to you?

Q: *What does "failure" mean to you?*

What do you want to hear?

A specific example to demonstrate what he or she means by "failure," not a lengthy philosophical discourse. This question offers you the opportunity to delve into mistakes and bad decisions, never a welcome topic for an interviewee. Look for honesty, a clear analysis of what went wrong, a willingness to admit responsibility (especially if they're taking responsibility for some aspects that weren't their fault), and the determination to change what caused it (or examples to show how it's already been transformed).

 Thumbs up

"Failure is not getting the job done when I have the means to do so. For example, once I was faced with a huge project. I should have realized at the outset that I didn't have the time. I must have been thinking there were 48 hours in a day! I also didn't have the knowledge I needed to do it correctly. Instead of asking some of the other people in my department for help, I blundered through. That won't ever happen to me again if I can help it!"

 Thumbs down

A wishy-washy, non-specific answer that forces you to ask too many follow-up questions.

Always remember the point of asking such open-ended questions: to get the candidate talking, hopefully revealing more than he would have if you had asked a more pointed question. So *keep quiet*. Feel free to nod, smile, or otherwise indicate you haven't fallen asleep. But avoid the temptation to fill those inevitable silences with your own stories. Staying silent during a pause is the most effective way to encourage the candidate to just keep talking—which is exactly what you want him or her to do.

Variations

◄ What does "weakness" mean to you?

◄ What does "competence" mean to you?

◄ What does "problem" mean to you?

◄ What does "untenable" mean to you?

◄ What does "disappointment" mean to you?

Q: *Do you believe we make our own luck? Tell me about the last time you did.*

What do you want to hear?

The successful candidate, whether she believes in luck (or the Tooth Fairy or the Easter Bunny), will welcome this question as an opportunity to demonstrate her initiative and motivation. Again, you expect the answer to describe a problem she faced, detail the actions taken, and the results achieved. What has she done to put herself in situations where good outcomes have occurred because she *worked* hard enough to get "lucky"?

Does the candidate believe this is an opportunity to tell you about the many risks she took with her current company's money? Thank her for the information…on her way out the door.

Q: *What would you say if I told you our interview is over?*

What do you want to hear?

You just lobbed a grenade. Maybe the candidate's first or second answers were so poor you are just trying to save some time and nudge him or her out the door. Maybe you are just baiting him or her, giving the candidate an opportunity to rise to the challenge of rejection. Maybe you just want to get back to work.

Whatever the reason, a candidate better be prepared to confront such unexpected aggression with a calm question of his or her own: "I'm sorry you feel that way. I thought I clearly expressed my passion for this position and why I believe I am very qualified for it. What part of my answer disappointed you?"

Variations

◄ What if I told you I thought this interview was off to a poor start?

◄ Sorry, you haven't convinced me you are remotely qualified for this position. We should end this interview now.

◄ Would you like to start over? You're not doing very well.

◄ I only have five more minutes. Why should I hire you?

You've started the conversation. Unless you have abruptly terminated the interview, there are many more specific questions to ask, starting with education.

6

QUESTIONS ABOUT THEIR EDUCATION

The more work experience a person has had, the less likely you will (or should) care about what he did in college, let alone high school. As important as particular courses and extracurricular leadership positions may have been a decade ago, no amount of educational success can take the place of solid, real-world, on-the-job experience.

What about an entry-level candidate who graduated months or even weeks earlier? How do you judge how she'll do on the job when her only (summer) job was intimately involved with salad ingredients? More important, how do you cut through the "creative" resumes that don't just "upgrade" insignificant experiences but attempt to blatantly transform a summer job at the local hot dog stand or on the beach into what sounds like a divisional vice presidency?

I presume you're seeking a well-rounded person who got decent grades but also has demonstrated desirable traits—leadership, team-building, writing, communicating—either through extracurricular activities, internships, and/or part-time work or volunteer experience. So be prepared to probe relentlessly to ensure that the glad grad in front of you doesn't cost you six months and thousands of dollars to train—right in time for her to move on to your competitor.

A candidate's resume should list not just a major and minor, but pertinent courses as well. And a savvy candidate will ensure that each resume is custom-produced so the particular courses that are included mesh as much as possible with the requirements of each specific job. The more technical the job, the easier it should be for you to determine whether the candidate has the pertinent training. But a liberal arts candidate may have little or no pertinent classwork, which means you have to make the connections yourself.

Here are some questions to get you started.

Q: *What extracurricular activities were you involved in?*

What do you want to hear?

I presume you're seeking a candidate who can demonstrate industriousness, not someone who did just enough to eke by. What the candidate has been doing—*whatever* the candidate has been doing—should show you a pattern that bears at least a passing resemblance to the job at hand. What he did during his summers, unless it was a pertinent internship or part-time job, is virtually irrelevant. He *chose* a major, a minor, courses, activities. You want to know the reasons why he made *those particular choices.* That will be the clearest indication of where his "real" interests lie, no matter the "objective" he's featured on his resume.

You're seeking enthusiasm, confidence, energy, dependability, honesty. A problem-solver. A team player. Someone who's willing to work hard to achieve difficult but worthy goals. How has everything this person did in college demonstrated her ability to become your ideal hire?

Your particular situation, job, company, and personal idiosyncrasies will affect how you compare campus activities to community work, other volunteer activities, and "real-world" work (especially if the student had to pay or help pay for school). You may emulate the draft philosophy of legendary football coach Bill Parcells—always pick the "best athlete," even if he plays a position at which you're already overstocked. Or prefer the alternative and "draft for need," accepting a less-qualified candidate simply because he plays the right position. Translation of this wandering metaphor: Seek someone who found a way to do it all.

 Thumbs up

Activities that bear some relationship to the job/industry, such as a college newspaper editor applying for a job in newspaper, book, or magazine publishing.

Activities that show a healthy balance, such as someone who participated in one or more sports *and* a cultural club (chess, theater, and so on) *and* a political club *and* who worked part-time, not someone whose focus was solely on a sport or cause, no matter how illustrious her athletic or other achievements.

A candidate who demonstrates the ability to manage multiple priorities (let's not forget coursework and maybe a part-time job here) and good time-management skills. (Unless, of course, you want a slightly obsessive, green-eye-shaded accountant who will add numbers for eight hours a day and believe he has the greatest job in the world. In that case, identify the candidate who was class treasurer and president of the Accounting Club.)

Here's a reasonable answer:

"I wish I'd had more time to write for the school paper. Whenever I wasn't studying, I pretty much had to work to pay for college. But I learned a number of things from the jobs I held that most people learn only after they've been in their careers for a while—such as how to work with other people and how to manage my time effectively."

 Thumbs down

Candidates who have spent an inordinate amount of time doing things outside of class but whose GPAs (grade point average) indicate they spent little time concentrating *in* class. Anything below a "B" average should lead you to ask a whole series of follow-up questions, forcing the candidate to explain "why."

Someone who seemingly has tried every activity at least once and has no clear direction. Why assume he'll suddenly change when you hire him?

Someone who thinks the perfect answer is a joke: "Well, John, I didn't do much more than drink beer and watch a lot of TV." I'm probably more appreciative of good jokes than the next guy, but an interview is simply the wrong place and the wrong time to tell them. Even if they're funny, you should question the common sense of anyone who thinks sitting across from your desk applying for a job is a good time and place to test a new stand-up routine.

Variations

◄   What made you choose those activities?

◄   Which ones did you most enjoy? Why?

◄   Which ones did you least enjoy? Why?

◄   Which ones do you regret *not* choosing? Why?

Clearly, there are no inherently right or wrong answers to these questions. You should continue probing in this manner to more fully reveal the way the candidate thinks, how she makes choices and decisions, and how flexible or inflexible she seems to be in those choices. Depending on your own circumstances, you will react positively or negatively to certain aspects of the impression these answers make, but you can't form an opinion without forcing the candidate to paint the picture.

Q: Why did you choose that college? Why did you choose your major? Why did you choose your minor? Which courses did you like most? Least?

What do you want to hear?

For someone just exiting college, this series of questions may well be substituted for the ubiquitous "So, tell me about yourself" and the many variations previously discussed.

If you are interviewing candidates for a highly technical job—engineering, science, programming, and so on—you should reasonably expect that they majored in engineering, the physical sciences, or computer science, and that their major and even minor coursework is pertinent. (Excepting someone like my friend Andy, who majored in astrophysics at MIT...and minored in theater.) If you're lucky, such a candidate will have demonstrated a particular interest in chemistry or computers or mechanical engineering while still in high school, making your task one of evaluating rather than creatively "transferring." (Hmm, that art history course shows analytical skills. Perfect for a computer analyst!)

Though not quite as technical, you bankers and Wall Street types should also have it easy if enough business administration, finance, and accounting majors and newly minted MBAs march in.

If only life were always so easy. More often than not, you will end up spending your days cajoling an endless line of history, English, and French lit majors to explain how their college education prepared them for a position with your firm.

What were they thinking? Did he or she choose a major because it was the easiest? Because it had specific relevance to other interests (demonstrated by consistent volunteer work or activities)? Because the candidate analyzed the job market and took courses to prepare for a particular career? Because they were there?

What other majors or minors did he or she consider? And why did he or she choose one and reject the others?

 Thumbs up

A candidate who talks about the skills she developed—writing ability, debating and language skills, math—especially in courses she didn't necessarily like or want to take. I *like* to hear that a candidate did well in a course she really didn't care for. Shouldn't you be looking for a new hire with that kind of attitude?

A non-technical candidate who nevertheless can demonstrate job- or career-related coursework.

Answers that deal with particular courses, not the specific workload or a professor's personality.

An acknowledgement that the candidate is well aware that, despite her *summa cum laude* credentials, she probably has less job-related knowledge than anybody at the company. Humility is an attractive trait at times, especially when it's well-deserved: "I know this position has its share of unpleasant duties, but I'm sure everyone who's had this job before me has learned a lot by doing them."

 Thumbs down

Blaming a professor, even tangentially, for a bad grade or experience should give you pause. Does this candidate have problems with authority figures?

Complaining about the workload of a course, semester, or year. You are seeking industriousness, not laziness.

There are times as an interviewer I have described in excruciating detail the worst or most mind-numbingly boring aspects of a job. A successful candidate shouldn't be fooled into expressing *any* negative reaction (even a raised eyebrow when "garbage detail" is being discussed). If you try a similar tactic, watch their body language. It will speak volumes.

Variations

◄ Why did you change majors? Change minors? Drop that course? Add that course?

◄ Does the candidate's explanation of why a change was made and the thinking that went into it make sense to you? Or was it simply to trade a difficult major for an easier one, a stratagem to take more classes with a girlfriend, or something you deem equally superfluous?

A candidate who has changed majors, perhaps more than once, must be ready to admit that his priorities and attitude changed over time. That once he started on the coursework for a particular major he quickly discovered it was not what he thought it would be. I suspect you (and many other interviewers) would find such candor refreshing and realistic. After all, how many teenagers know that eventually they will (or want to) become accountants, hospital administrators, loading dock foremen, or, for that matter, interviewers for human resources? But you should expect such interviewees to be ready to convincingly demonstrate how their other studies contributed to making them the best candidates for the job.

Q: Why are you applying for a job in a field other than your major?

What do you want to hear?

If a candidate is applying for a technical sales position, but majored in art history, this is an obvious question. The answer should be brief and positive—she has reexamined her career goals, enjoys customer contact, and appreciates (and welcomes) the competitive nature of sales. Not to mention that there are virtually no actual jobs available to her in art history. Are there particular things an art historian must learn that directly translate into sales? Particular skills? You should certainly ask the questions you need to find out.

Just because so many students who major in more esoteric areas are, by definition, ill-prepared for some specific jobs (and many people are changing jobs, industries, and even careers far more frequently), does *not* mean that you cannot and should not put such candidates on the spot. Make them sell you on how their learning will benefit *you*.

Q: *If you were starting college tomorrow, what courses would you take?*

What do you want to hear?

A bit of candor, but certainly not a dissertation involving a wholesale change of major, courses, and hair color. You may sympathize with an interviewee's teen-aged *angst*, but should certainly expect that he or she has commenced "adulting."

 Thumbs up

A good candidate should detail changes he would have made in his course selections that would have made him a better candidate for this job. Should he have taken more marketing courses, an accounting course, a statistics seminar? If it's clear to you from the job description that he would have benefited from some such change, it would be nice to hear him state it. He should also not be afraid to admit that it took him a while to find the right course of study. You've also given him a good opportunity to describe how courses that are completely unrelated to this or any other "real-world" career nevertheless were valuable in his development.

 Thumbs down

◄ Anyone who claims they would have gone away to school so they could have dated more.

◄ Anyone who answers, "Same courses, but this time I'd pass them."

◄ Anyone whose answers clearly do not indicate an understanding of the *purpose* of the question—generously giving her an opportunity to show she knows what the job entails and, because of that understanding, would have taken more pertinent courses (while dropping that full-year 17th-century Chinese literature course like a hot chopstick).

Q: *What did you learn from the internships on your resume?*

What do you want to hear?

You, of course, don't really believe that any new hire, especially an entry-level candidate, is going to make a significant (or even measurable) contribution to your company right away. Training and experience will be necessary to make him or her productive. So when facing an inexperienced candidate, you should try to determine how "trainable" he or she appears to be.

 Thumbs up

◄ A candidate who shows how the internship experiences she has had complement her academic training.

◄ Pertinent internships that directly relate to his new job/career.

◄ Well-thought-out answers that demonstrate career concerns.

◄ Good recommendations from internship supervisors.

Thumbs down

◀ Anyone who sincerely believes—and actually implies—that college is where she learned the "secret of life." No one likes a know-it-all, especially a very young one.

◀ No internships in a field in which they are *de rigueur*.

◀ Internships in an unrelated field, especially if many courses/activities are in that same field, which implies the candidate's *real* area of interest lies elsewhere.

◀ Poor or no recommendation from his internship supervisor or a negative reaction from the candidate about its value. Even if his internship tested nothing but his copier skills, a smart interviewee would never introduce such a negative into the interview.

Variations

◀ Why are there no internships on your resume?

◀ Why weren't any of your internships paid?

◀ Would you repeat each of your internships?

◀ Why did you pick those particular internships?

◀ Why did you feel the need to do an internship?

◀ Have your ever shadowed a professional in this field?

Q: *In what courses did you get the worst grades? How do you think that will affect your performance on this job?*

What do you want to hear?

You should ask to see copies of their college transcripts if they make it past the first hurdle, but in the meantime, you can certainly get a taste of what you'd find there. There may be some surprises in store, like the person applying for that financial assistant job who barely passed every accounting and math course he took.

Should you expect that every interviewee is a straight-A student and, therefore, will have a hard time answering this question? Not in my world. So the answer to the first part of the question is less important than the explanation and how the interviewee handles introducing a negative: "Yes sir, I eventually dropped Statistical Analysis 101, but it was a course completely outside my major and, as far as I know, has nothing to do with the job you're offering."

 Thumbs up

◄ Anyone who really can't answer the question because they didn't get any bad grades! (Please send them over to me first. I'll take care of them.)

◄ An answer that satisfactorily explains the one or two less-than-stellar grades. If the poor grade was in an elective course, a smart candidate will blame the extra time he spent on his major (in which, of course, he did great). If he did poorly in a major course, perhaps outside activities were to blame (and the candidate has a ready and believable explanation for placing such activities ahead of good grades).

Thumbs down

◄ Too many Cs and Ds to count.

◄ No reasonable explanation, leading you to assume that the candidate simply didn't care or isn't all that bright.

◄ A choice that the candidate made whose wisdom you question. Although it may have been quite exciting and educational to devote a significant amount of time to getting a friend elected class president, was that plethora of Ds a viable tradeoff?

Variations

◄ Are grades a good measure of ability?

◄ Why didn't you get better grades?

◄ Why are your grades so erratic?

◄ What happened that semester (year) when your grades sank?

Again, if the candidate's grades were great, he or she should be suitably proud; if they weren't, hopefully there were mitigating circumstances—work, an unusual opportunity, a family crisis, whatever. If he or she fails to take responsibility for a poor performance, consider it a thumbs down. And if he or she gets defensive, you may reasonably question whether he or she actually *made* a choice or simply acted without considering the consequences of that action. Pertinent follow-up questions should be obvious based on each candidate's response.

7

QUESTIONS ABOUT THEIR
WORK EXPERIENCE

You've established your interviewing criteria by considering such important applicant details as college internships and grades, especially for those who graduated less than a few years ago. Now the bigger questions need to be asked: If the applicant graduated some time ago, what has he been doing out here in the real world?

Do you believe past performance is a reasonable predictor of future performance? You probably do, which is why you are about to embark on a series of questions to learn more about the candidate's on-the-job experience.

Q: Tell me about your last three positions.

What do you want to hear?

This is a question designed to see how well the candidate organizes what could be a lot of data into a brief, coherent overview of three, five, 10, or more years' experience. It will help you to flesh out the resume, catch inconsistencies, create a roadmap for the far more detailed inquiries to follow, and evaluate how well the candidate attempts to "edit" answers in order to match his or her experience and skills to the job at hand.

 Thumbs up

◄ Pertinent experience and skills described in a brief, coherent, positive answer.

◄ A candidate cognizant of the importance of connecting *her* experience and skills to *your* job requirements.

◄ A career demonstrating a pattern of increasingly greater responsibility, authority, money, subordinates, skill level, and so on.

 Thumbs down

◄ "What exactly do you want to know?" (Answer: What I just asked for!)

◄ Any complaints about bosses, subordinates, and/or coworkers. You're seeking a responsible individual, no matter what the position, so why would you be impressed by someone attempting to blame everyone else for his failures? Interviewees should know that *even if they weren't at fault*, you're probably not going to deem any transfer of blame a positive.

◄ Lateral moves (why wasn't he or she promoted?) or, even more so, clear demotions.

◄ A candidate's inability to clearly answer the question or assemble all the experiences into a coherent whole.

You would think no one would refer to a job that doesn't appear on his or her resume, but it happens all the time. (Follow up: "Your resume says that you were working at _____ in 2013, but you just said you were working at _____. Can you explain?")

I will admit to being part of the stupidest interview ever undertaken by an otherwise smart, reasonably experienced person. I spent the first five years after college graduation trying to be a full-time writer without actually starving to death. The only way I could accomplish this was to write for hours a day while working a series of short-term, part-time jobs—often two or three at once. I had dozens of jobs. Some lasted a day, some weeks or months, one for nearly two years.

When I interviewed for my first *full*-time job, the only job that appeared on my resume was the two years typing manuscripts at a trade association, because my supervisor allowed me to describe it as a full-time job, and one I had had for the full five years.

Within minutes of greeting the interviewer for a major magazine company, I was proudly discoursing on what I had learned at two or three of my short-term jobs. Yes, the ones that officially didn't exist.

The interviewer and I reached the same conclusion simultaneously: I wasn't getting the job or, for that matter, any other potential job at that magazine company.

So don't be surprised if an otherwise-promising candidate steps in the same mud puddle as I did. You may be more or less forgiving that the editor who showed me the door.

Q: *What was your favorite job? Why?*

What do you want to hear?

This is a wonderful question because an unsuspecting candidate may forget it is an interview question and blurt out the truth:

"My favorite job was at WPRB radio. It was very loose and informal and there was little supervision, which I really enjoyed. I had the freedom to program my own shows with little or no interference and only had to put in 20 hours a week to actually get my work done, so the rest of the time I could write or think up new creative ideas."

Very nice, except the successful applicant will be assisting three high-powered businesspeople at a highly structured and very rigid old-line firm.

Next!

 Thumbs up

◄ An answer that describes a job very much like the one you are trying to fill.

 Thumbs down

Any answer that is clearly at odds with the job at hand. The problem isn't that someone's last job offered some travel and this one doesn't, or a previous position offered more varied tasks and this one is more highly focused, even if either happens to be the case. The problem for you is that this answer *failed to take into account what the current job entails,* which should indicate to you a lack of pre-interview research or the simple inability to realize the importance of matching his past experience to your needs.

Also, a job that a candidate identifies as a favorite for reasons you consider frivolous.

Q: Tell me about the best boss you ever had. Tell me about the worst one.

What do you want to hear?

A smart candidate should attempt to describe *you* (as the best one, of course)! After all, that's what you'd *really* like to hear, isn't it? Someone just as wonderful, helpful, motivating, and cheerful as *you*. Presuming the candidate is not clairvoyant enough to understand that you expect him to suck up quite that blatantly, at least you should hear that he most enjoyed working for someone who was interested in helping him learn and grow, involved in monitoring his progress, and generous about giving credit when and where it was due.

Worst boss? Beware the candidate who gets carried away with venomous accusations. They should serve only to introduce doubt about the candidate's competence or ability to get along with other people.

For example, if she claims her boss favored other employees over her, you might wonder *why* her boss liked other employees more. If he complains about a boss who was always looking over his shoulder, you might wonder whether it was because he couldn't be trusted to complete a task accurately, on budget, on time—or all three. (Which is why he "quit.")

Any negativity that arises from this question could lead to some pointed follow-up questions to give the candidate a chance to salvage what is left of an interview gone bad. Or you could just thank him or her and move on.

Thumbs up

A "favorite" boss who is close in style and personality to the person you know the candidate will be working for.

Any interviewee who correctly interprets this question as another opportunity to highlight her own experiences, accomplishments, and aptitudes. There are bad bosses out there, but a savvy candidate should be able to put a supervisor's failures in a positive context. For example, if a previous boss was "stingy with his knowledge," the candidate can use that example to emphasize her desire to learn. Likewise, an "uninvolved" supervisor could be cited by someone who desires to work within a cohesive team.

 Thumbs down

Any negativity.

Any attempt to blame the boss for failures, such as:

"You know, I had to really work hard to learn how to sell spice racks in the South Pacific, but it sure didn't help that my boss had never sold a darn thing to anyone. She seemed to think that everything I did was wrong and constantly called me out of the field for 'evaluations.' I spent so much time filling out unnecessary reports for her and attending meetings to discuss why I wasn't reaching my unrealistic quota that I never had a chance to succeed. I hope my new boss just leaves me alone."

Q: Is there anything you could have done to improve your relationship with that supervisor?

 Thumbs up

Of course there was (unless the candidate is too dense to scramble aboard the life raft you've just flung overboard). His subsequent work experience has shown him how to better accept criticism. Now that he has a better understanding of the pressures supervisors are under, he can more successfully anticipate their needs. The candidate should welcome this opportunity to demonstrate his or her experience, perceptiveness, and maturity.

 Thumbs down

"Nah, not with that dumb so-and-so. He reveled in our misery. I'm glad we trolled him!"

Q: What were the most memorable accomplishments at your last job? In your career?

What do you want to hear?

A good answer should focus on the most recent accomplishments, but only those that are relevant to the position for which the candidate is interviewing.

For example, a friend of mine who had been an editor for years answered this question by talking at length about the times she'd been asked to write promotional copy for the marketing department. She was trying to change careers, so she tried to shift the interviewer's attention from her editing experience to her strengths and accomplishments as a marketing copywriter.

113

A successful candidate should be able to explain why she was able to achieve these peaks in her career. For example:

"I really stopped to listen to what my customers wanted, rather than just trying to sell them."

"I realized I needed to know a lot more about Subchapter-S corporations, so I enrolled in a tax seminar."

This type of response tells you the interviewee has given a great deal of thought to how she will reach her realistic goals, rather than blindly plunging ahead in their general direction. By letting you know that she is in the practice of regularly assessing her shortcomings, a savvy candidate shows that she is better able to find the means to overcome them.

 Thumbs down

◄ Bragging about accomplishments that have nothing to do with the requirements for this job.

◄ Citing frivolous, meaningless, minor, or dubious accomplishments:

  ◁ "I finally managed to get out of bed every morning and get to work on time."

  ◁ "I raised $25 for the volunteer fire department."

  ◁ "I managed to cut my coffee intake by 15 percent."

Q: What is the biggest failure in your career? What steps did you take to make sure it doesn't happen again?

What do you want to hear?

On the one hand, you're inviting the unwary interviewee to view you as a priest and your office as a confessional, encouraging him to produce a detailed log of his every shortcoming, misstep, and misdeed. Even a modestly intelligent candidate should have learned by now that introducing *any* negativity into an interview is *verboten*.

It would be equally silly for a candidate to pretend she's never experienced failure in the course of her career, education, or life. So you're clearly forcing her to at least *introduce* a negative. What you're really seeking is an answer to the *second* part of the question: "Hey, we've all failed, but what did you *do* about it the last time you did?"

 Thumbs up

A failure for which the candidate does not appear to be fully responsible. (When I'm interviewing, a successful candidate scores the most points by making it obvious she wasn't fully responsible for a debacle but is ready to shoulder the blame anyway.)

A job-related failure, with the candidate convincing you he or she now recognizes what the error was and offering you concrete examples that illustrate the lessons he or she has learned.

 Thumbs down

◄ A candidate who claims she has never failed at anything.

◄ A candidate who cites a non-work-related failure, especially a frivolous or dubious one.

◄ No evidence he or she has taken responsibility for whatever failure is cited and no evidence that any changes were made as a result.

◄ A candidate who declares "it can never happen again," an unrealistic assessment that should lead you to question his judgement.

◄ A candidate who actually admits a huge work-related weakness: "I've always hated my bosses, every one. But I think I'll like you!"

Variations

◄ What's your greatest weakness?

◄ What's the worst decision you ever made?

◄ What's the dumbest thing you ever did?

◄ What would you say is the biggest problem you've failed to overcome so far?

◄ What don't you want me to know about you?

◄ What aren't you telling me?

When asking any or all of these questions, you must continually probe, always seeking more details.

If a candidate says his greatest weakness is a fear of delegating because it always seems he can get it done faster and better himself, you might ask, "Tell me about the last time you should have delegated but didn't. What happened? Would you do it that way again? Would you do it differently today?"

Consistent probing—especially when you've asked negative types of questions—may well reveal weaknesses, failures, and problems the candidate would prefer to forget about.

Probing can also help you assess the candidate's character: how she reacts to stress; how well she handles pressure, failure, or success; her own standards of "success" and "failure"; and how willing she is to assume responsibility, especially for decisions or outcomes that weren't her fault.

Q: *Have you managed people in any of the positions you've held?*

What do you want to hear?

Moving up in most companies and careers means managing people, so even if you're not hiring this person for a managerial position, I assume you would like to hear a "yes." This would, at the very least, assure you that someone else has trusted the candidate enough to give him *some* responsibility, if only for a single, part-time assistant.

Clearly an entry-level candidate answering "no" shouldn't be branded "non-management" material because of a lack of such experience. But I'd give points to any recent graduate smart enough to consider "leadership" and "management" synonymous and list the clubs and other activities in which she "managed" members or volunteers, or built consensus within the group.

If he does have some experience, you will obviously want to know specific details about how many people were supervised and in what capacities they worked.

 Thumbs up

◄ Not just management experience, but managing the same (or a slightly higher) number of people in a similarly sized and directed department or division.

◄ A positive appreciation of the varying skills needed to manage and motivate different types of employees, especially if the applicant never actually managed anyone "on the job."

Thumbs down

◄ No management experience for a job that requires they manage people. (Remember: A "thumbs down" urges you to stop and think, not automatically eliminate a candidate. If we only hired people who have managed others, how would we ever grow our own stars? And who's to say that previous management experience isn't going to consist of a lot of *bad* management experience?)

◄ Any negative expression of management experience: "Yes, I managed two people at the last firm and let me tell you, they were both overpaid do-nothings!"

◄ A candidate who appears to underestimate the requirements of management, thinking it's just an increase in prestige and money but not appreciating the pressures of increased responsibility, new skills needed, and so on.

◄ A candidate who seems unwilling to work to acquire the skills necessary to successfully manage people.

Q: *What makes a good leader?*

What do you want to hear?

A great leader knows how to motivate each team member or subordinate—welcoming ideas, nourishing and encouraging creativity, and establishing a culture of mutual respect.

She enthusiastically takes charge without overpowering others' contributions, interactions, or participation. Convinced she must be a role model for her organization, she nevertheless finds ways to empower her subordinates and maximize their efforts and results.

Presuming a candidate includes most or all of these traits in his answer, you will want him to cite specific examples in which he exemplified them.

Variations

◄ Tell me about a time you helped a subordinate achieve his or her goals.

◄ Give me an example when your leadership abilities were vital components of your team's success.

◄ Have you ever been responsible for training anyone?

◄ What do you do when you have to "take charge"?

◄ How do you persuade people to do something they don't want to do?

◄ How do you decide what to delegate and to whom?

◄ What are the most important qualities you believe a leader must possess?

Q: *How do you motivate people?*

What do you want to hear?

A good answer will note how it "depends on the person," then offer one or two concrete examples. A poor candidate will imply that all people are motivated by the same thing or can be motivated with the same approach. This also is a good follow-up question to "What is your management philosophy?"

Variations

◄ Tell me about the last time you had to get others to support one of your ideas.

◄ Tell me about someone who achieved success because of your help.

◄ Tell me about the last time you had to deal with a particularly difficult employee.

◄ Tell me about the last time you had to sell an unpopular idea or task to your team, subordinates, or boss.

Q: *Tell me about the types of people you have trouble getting along with.*

What do you want to hear?

This is an excellent follow-up question to the previous one, especially if the candidate has indicated great skill at managing and/or motivating people, because it seemingly requires a negative response. This could be a landmine for a candidate who responds too quickly, answering "pushy, abrasive people" only to find out later that you're known for being "brusque."

One person I interviewed gave me what I thought was a good answer to this question:

"I was discussing this problem with my boss just the other day. He told me I'm too impatient with slow performers. He told me that the world is filled with 'C' rather than 'A' or 'B' people, and I expected them all to be great performers. So I guess I do have trouble with mediocre and poor workers. I don't expect to ever accept poor work, but I'm learning to be more patient."

Was he *really* discussing this "just the other day"? Did the conversation ever take place? Probably not, but who cares?

Shouldn't anyone you're seeking to hire be impatient with slow performers? He even discussed what he's doing to solve his "problem." Short and sweet, but very much to the point.

 Thumbs down

You know the identity of the candidate's boss and with whom he'll be working. If he has trouble with detailed, organized accounting types—a good description of you, his new boss, and everybody you work with—need I say more?

A general, vague answer, supplying little detail—no matter how much you probe or urge—indicates both a lack of analysis and a dearth of self-knowledge. Of course, candidates don't really want to answer this question—which is why you asked it. But they certainly should expect that it or one of its brethren will be on the agenda: "What's your greatest weakness?" "Tell me about your worst boss." "Tell me about your greatest failure."

Variations

◄ What types of people have trouble getting along with you?

◄ How do you deal with people you don't like?

◄ How do you deal with people who don't like you?

◄ Do you think it's important that your subordinates like you?

◄ Is a friendly relationship with your boss important to you?

◄ How much of your job satisfaction is dependent on your work relationships?

These are great follow-up questions, especially if the answer to the previous question was vague or wishy-washy. You're continuing to probe, and you're not going to stop 'til you hit a nerve. Even if the answer to the previous question was reasonable, any of these follow-up questions might uncover some inconsistencies (meaning the candidate anticipated the first question and prepared for it, but was ill-prepared for any corollary or follow-up question).

A smart candidate will be ready with examples that are unverifiable—tales from companies that have disappeared, former bosses now unreachable, decisions long forgotten. At the very least, their stories will be about coworkers or subordinates, not supervisors who could attest to (or challenge) their veracity.

Q: You've changed jobs quite frequently. How do we know you'll stick around?

What do you want to hear?

As you well know, the hiring process is expensive for your company and time-consuming for you. Job-hoppers only serve to make it a more frequent process, which you probably wish to avoid. So you're seeking someone who can convince you that your company and the position you're offering is their very own Promised Land.

 Thumbs up

A successful candidate will probably either confess that he had some difficulty defining his career goals at first, but now is quite sure of his direction, or convince you that she left previous positions only after realizing that moving on was the only way to increase her responsibilities and broaden her experience.

Sherri had four jobs in the first six years after college graduation. Her clever reply to an interviewer's skepticism about her staying power combines both techniques:

"All through college, I was convinced that I wanted to be a programmer. But after a few months in my first job, I found that I was unhappy. Naturally, I blamed the company and the job. So when an opportunity opened up at Lakeside Bank, I grabbed it. But not long after the initial euphoria wore off, I was unhappy again.

"By this time I'd noticed that I really did enjoy the part of my job that dealt with applications. So when I heard about the job in end-user computing at Safe Invest, I went for it. I learned a lot there, until I hit a 'glass ceiling.' It was a small firm, so there was no place for me to grow.

"I was recruited for the applications position at Deep Pockets Bank, and I got the job because of some of the innovations I'd developed at SI. The work has been terrific. But once again, I find that I'm a one-person department.

"This position offers the opportunity to manage a department and interact with programmers, coders, and applications specialists on the cutting edge of technology. Throughout my career, the one thing that has remained constant is my love of learning. This job would give me the chance to learn so much."

Variation

◄ You have been with your current employer a short amount of time. Is this an indication that you'll be moving around a lot throughout your career?

Q: You've been with the same organization for __ years. Won't you have a tough time getting used to a different culture and structure?

What do you want to hear?

This is the corollary of the previous question. Pity the poor candidate: If he's moved around, you question his staying power.

If she stuck with a single company, you question her initiative. *C'est la vie.*

During the candidate's stint with his current company, he's probably worked for more than one boss. He may even have supervised many different types of people in various departments. Certainly he's teamed up with a variety of coworkers. And from inside his organization, he's had a chance to observe a wide variety of *other* organizations—competitors, vendors, customers, and so on. He's flexible—and loyal—and should emphasize to you that this is a valuable combination.

Variation

◄ You've been with your current employer for only a short amount of time. Is this an indication that you'll soon be moving on from our company?

By the time you've asked your introductory questions, questions about high school and college experiences, and these preliminary "on-the-job" questions, you should certainly have an idea of whether a candidate is truly viable.

If she has impressed you every step of the way, keep on reading—there are more questions to make sure you've found your new hire. If he is clearly wrong for the position, you can save yourself some time and move on.

If you still don't know, it's time to ask even more detailed questions.

8

QUESTIONS ABOUT STYLE
AND SUBSTANCE

In the world of business, "style" has little to do with how well you dress (although at some companies, and in some positions, the right wardrobe may be a defining element of the culture). Typically, your business style is a measure—often a subjective one, at that—of how you conduct yourself on the job.

How well do the candidates you're considering get along with superiors? Subordinates? Peers? What's their management philosophy? Do they prefer to work by themselves or with others? You want to know how they'll act and interact once they're on the job, and these "style" questions are your informational tickets.

Although you are certainly trying to be as objective as possible in evaluating each candidate you interview, you will undoubtedly base at least some of your hiring decisions on your feelings about each candidate's attitude. In every case, you are assessing how the candidate's style fits in with the organizational culture, your own style, and/or the team's style. So, in general, a "thumbs up" is any answer that seems to indicate a positive fit, and a "thumbs down" should accompany any substantive differences of style that you feel may cause problems. For the most part, this makes your assessment of any candidate's answers highly subjective. Rather than characterizing an answer as inherently right or wrong, you are simply trying to ascertain whether he or she will get along with Joe or Sally or Jimmy—the other members of the company, department, or team.

Following is a series of style questions you may choose to ask at any point during the interview:

Q: Are you an organized person?

What do you want to hear?

Even if *you* firmly believe that a neat desk is the sign of a sick mind, you want the candidate to talk in detail about the organizational skills that she has developed—time management, project management, needs assessment, delegation—and how those skills have made her more effective. I'd be wary of a candidate who veers too closely to either extreme. I don't want to hire someone so anal-retentive that he always knows the number of paper clips in his drawer or one so *dis*organized that it would take him most of the morning to *find* a paper clip.

Variations

◄ Paint me a mental picture of your current office.

◄ Describe the top of your desk.

◄ Tell me about the first five files in your file cabinet.

◄ Does your smartphone help you stay organized? What apps do you use?

◄ Do you use an online calendar? Which one?

◄ What organizational aids do you use on a daily basis?

◄ How do you establish priorities?

◄ How do you handle multiple priorities?

◄ Tell me about the last time you just couldn't get everything done.

◄ Have you ever forgotten an important appointment or deadline?

◄ Tell me about a time you got too involved with one aspect of a project and the whole suffered.

Q: *Do you manage your time well?*

What do you want to hear?

I hope the candidate can truthfully say that he is a self-starter and (almost) never procrastinates. And, if he *can't* say it truthfully, I hope he's smart enough to realize now is not the time to wail about his broken alarm clock—which is why, by the way, he was 15 minutes late for the interview, remember? Good employees are able to set goals, prioritize tasks, and devote appropriate amounts of time to each.

In answering a rather conceptual question like this one (and what could be more conceptual than time?), a savvy candidate should try to sprinkle in specifics. Here are a few examples:

"I rarely miss a deadline. When circumstances beyond my control interfere, I make up the time lost as quickly as possible."

"I establish a to-do list first thing in the morning. Then I add to it—and reprioritize tasks, if necessary—as the day goes on."

"I really like interacting with the people I work with. But when I need to focus on detailed tasks, I make sure to set aside time that will be free of interruptions of any kind, so I can concentrate and work more effectively."

Variations

◄ Tell me about the first 60 minutes of a typical day.

◄ What are the first three things you do most mornings?

◄ How often do you stay late to complete your work?

◄ What time-management tools do you use on a daily basis?

◄ Tell me about a time your time-management skills positively affected an outcome.

◄ What have you done to make more effective use of your time?

◄ What does your typical daily schedule look like?

◄ How much time do you spend planning rather than doing?

◄ What is your biggest time-waster?

Q: How do you handle change?

What do you want to hear?

Business is *about* change. In order to remain competitive, we have to adapt to changes in technology, personnel, leadership, business structure, the types of services we deliver, or the products we produce. So you would expect a successful candidate to be flexible, willing, and able to adapt.

Only you know the kind of changes your company goes through on a weekly or monthly basis. If you are a fast-growing entrepreneurial firm, "change" is your middle name. Someone otherwise super-qualified but addicted to security and structure will soon flounder. A candidate more comfortable in a fast-moving, make-decisions-by-the-seat-of-your-pants kind of atmosphere might be the right hire, even if she lacks other credentials.

A good candidate should choose an example of a change she faced that resulted in something positive, trying to show that she not only accepted change and adapted to it, but flourished as a result of it.

Variations

◄ Tell me about a time you had to work with someone who had a radically different style of working.

◄ Tell me about a time you had to change the way you worked to successfully achieve a result.

◄ Tell me about the last project during which you had to "change horses in midstream."

◄ Tell me about a change that affected your ability to complete a task or reach a goal.

◄ Tell me about a time you had to remain flexible and adaptive in order to achieve a result.

Q: How do you go about making important decisions?

What do you want to hear?

Presuming that quite a few questions have already gone by, a good candidate should already have some sense, both from his own research and from the previous questions, of your company's particular culture. He should shade his answer to this question accordingly.

Meanwhile, *you* need to think in terms of your main concerns when evaluating his answer. You know the position for which you are hiring. Will the successful candidate need to be analytical? Creative? Willing to call on the expertise of others? Able to work alone? To travel on a moment's notice?

You might hope to hear something like this:

"When I'm faced with an important decision, I ask the advice of others. I try to consider everything. But ultimately, I'm the one who decides. I guess that's why they say, 'It's lonely at the top.' The higher you go in management, the more responsibility you have and the more decisions you have to make by yourself."

This is an acceptable general answer, but you will probably want to probe for detail. Ask something like, "Tell me about the last important decision you had to make, how you went about making it, and the results you achieved." Does the candidate's example support the generalities she just espoused? Or does she inadvertently show she does things completely differently—better or worse—than she just said she did?

Variations

◄ Give me an example of a difficult decision you recently made.

◄ What was the biggest decision you ever made in your career?

◄ How important is logic in your decision-making?

◄ What input do your subordinates have when you have to make a decision?

◄ Tell me about the best decision you made in your last job. What else could you have done? Was your decision the best of those options?

◄ On what basis do you generally choose between competing alternatives?

◄ Tell me about the last time you knew you had made the wrong decision but didn't/wouldn't admit it until you were forced to.

Q: Do you work well under pressure?

What do you want to hear?

You will expect everyone to say "yes" to this question (and probably eliminate anyone foolish enough to say "no"). However, you will probe and make candidates provide examples that support their claims to chillness. Be wary of candidates who choose anecdotes that imply that the pressure they've faced has resulted from their own procrastination or failure to anticipate problems.

Variations

◄ What do you do to handle or reduce stress?

◄ How do you handle frustration?

◄ Tell me about a time you were under extreme pressure but successfully met your goals.

◄ Tell me about the last time pressure led you to indecision, a poor decision, or a mistake. What would you have done differently? Have you found yourself in a similar situation since? What did you do?

◄ What was the most stressful situation you've faced and how did you deal with it?

◄ Tell me about the last time you were frustrated.

◄ Tell me about the last time you were impatient.

◄ Tell me about the last time you made a rash decision.

◄ Tell me about the last time you were indecisive.

◄ Tell me about the last time you lost confidence.

The questioning pattern I am recommending throughout this book should be apparent by now: probe, probe, then probe some more. A candidate can only rehearse so many generalizations and remember a limited number of little white lies. The more detailed your questions, the more likely they will expose any misrepresentations, exaggerations, or omissions. And in doing so, you will continue to add multi-hued brush strokes to each candidate's portrait.

Q: Do you anticipate problems well or merely react to them?

What do you want to hear?

All managers panic from time to time. The best learn to protect themselves by anticipating problems that might be lurking just around the corner. For example, one sales manager I know had his staff provide weekly reports on both positive and negative budget variances. By sharing this valuable information with his boss and the manufacturing, distribution, and marketing arms of the company, he helped improve product turnover and boost flagging sales. This kind of story is terrific fodder for successful interviews and the kind of example you should expect to hear.

Variations

◄ Tell me how you approach a difficult problem.

◄ What was the biggest problem you faced at your last job?

◄ Tell me about a problem that required careful and extensive analysis. How did you approach it? What did you do?

◄ What procedures have you initiated to help your employees solve problems on their own?

Q: *Are you a risk-taker or do you prefer to play it safe?*

What do you want to hear?

You are probing for intimations of innovation and creativity. Is he the shepherd or just one of the flock? But you also want to find out whether he might turn into a "loose cannon" that will ignore company policies and be all too ready to lead a fatal cavalry charge.

Variations

◄ Tell me about the last time you took a risk. Was it the right decision? What should you have done differently?

◄ Tell me about the last time you played it safe. Did you miss an opportunity or avoid a debacle?

◄ Tell me about a time playing it safe turned out to be wrong or, at least, less successful.

◄ Tell me about the riskiest decision you have ever made.

Q: *If you could start your career over again, what would you do differently?*

What do you want to hear?

The savvy candidate should quote Paul Anka (via Sinatra): "Regrets? I've had a few. But all in all, too few to mention."

But listen carefully to *which* regrets are mentioned and what the candidate claims to have learned as a result. Did he leave his first job because he was too impatient for a promotion, only to realize he hadn't learned all he could have? Did she miss the opportunity to specialize in some area or develop a particular expertise that she should have?

 Thumbs up

"My only regret is that I didn't go in this direction sooner. I started my career in editorial, and I enjoyed that. But once I got into marketing, I found I really loved it. Now, I can't wait to get to work every day."

 Thumbs down

"I wish I had never gotten into magazine publishing in the first place. But now I guess I'm stuck. And to think, I could have been blogging every day and hosting a weekly podcast...."

Variations

◄ What was the biggest mistake you ever made when choosing a job?

◄ How important has money been in your career choices?

Q: *Do you prefer to work by yourself or with others?*

What do you want to hear?

Again, the position for which you're hiring will dictate how you should expect a candidate to shape his or her answer to this question. Let's presume you're trying to hire an on-the-road sales rep who may develop an unhealthy crush on his or her rental car but will otherwise interact solely with customers, waitresses, and hotel employees. You won't want to hear that a candidate thrives on her relationships with coworkers and can't imagine working without a lot of interaction.

Even if a candidate does like the interaction at work, she shouldn't try to paint her environment as a bed of roses without thorns. You know the saying: "You can choose your friends, but you can't choose your relatives." That goes for coworkers, too.

Every job situation forces us to get along with people we might not choose to socialize with. But we must get along with them and, quite often, for long stretches of time and under difficult circumstances. A successful candidate will acknowledge this reality and confidently talk about how he or she has managed to get along with a wide variety of other people.

Variations

◄   How do you get along with your superior(s)? With your coworkers? With your subordinates?

◄   How much time per week do you spend working alone? Do you think it should be more or less?

◄   Do you enjoy doing individual research?

◄   Do you tend to procrastinate when left alone?

The answers to these questions should, first of all, bear some relation to the answers to earlier questions about people with whom the candidate has had trouble or those who have had trouble getting along with him or her. But this is, again, a highly cultural question, and one in which the requirements of the job define the "rightness" of any answer. If a candidate thrives working alone but you're hiring someone who will always be part of a team, the dichotomy will be obvious.

Q: *How do you handle conflict?*

What do you want to hear?

"I really don't get angry with other people very often. I'm usually able to work things out or anticipate problems before they occur. When conflicts can't be avoided, I don't back down. But I certainly do try to be reasonable."

"I've had confrontations with coworkers who weren't holding up their end of a job. I feel that employees owe it to their bosses, customers, and coworkers to do their jobs properly."

Variations

◄ Tell me about the last time you had to resolve a problem between team members or coworkers.

◄ Tell me about the last time you had a conflict with your boss. What did you do to resolve it?

◄ How do you keep a positive attitude?

◄ Is conflict inevitable?

◄ Tell me about a difficult situation you handled poorly. Why did you choose that approach? What did you learn? What happened as a result?

◄ Tell me about how you handled a particularly difficult coworker or employee.

◄ Tell me about the last time you took an unpopular stand. How did you handle others who disagreed with your position?

Q: *How do you behave when you have a problem with a coworker?*

What do you want to hear?

"I had to work with a designer who just refused to listen to any of my suggestions. He would answer me in monosyllables and then drag his feet before doing anything I requested. Finally I said, 'Look, we're both professionals. Neither of us has the right answer all the time. I have noticed that you don't really like my suggestions. But rather than resist implementing them, why don't we just discuss what you don't like?' That worked like a charm. We even became friends."

Variations

◄ Tell me about the last time you lost your temper.

◄ How often do you get angry?

◄ What in particular makes you angry?

◄ How do you deal with difficult people?

◄ Tell me about the last time you disagreed with your boss. A coworker. A subordinate. What did you do, and what was the result?

◄ Tell me about the last time you had to deal with an irate customer, vendor, or client.

Q: *Tell me about the last time you were asked to do something you thought was inappropriate.*

What do you want to hear?

First and foremost, you want to understand what this candidate deems inappropriate. Does she bristle about the time she was asked to make coffee? Or was she put in an untenable position by a boss or company with low ethical standards? You may consider the former a minor occurrence…unless you know her new boss is prone to such politically incorrect requests. If she were asked to "cook the books," sell defective products, or cover up illegalities, you will want to know all the details and could ask a long series of probing questions. If a major ethical lapse occurred some time ago, you will definitely want to know why she is still working at that company.

Variations

◄ Tell me about the last time you saw a boss, coworker, employee, or team member do something inappropriate, unethical, or dishonest.

◄ Give me an example of a time you exercised good judgment.

◄ Tell me about a time you were honest or ethical even though the consequences were potentially onerous.

◄ Tell me about the last time you covered up a mistake.

◄ When was the last time you covered up someone else's mistake?

◄ Tell me about a time you had to deal with company politics.

◄ Have you ever taken credit for someone else's work?

◄ Tell me about the last time you lied to your boss.

◄ How much time do you spend doing personal business while at work?

If integrity is a major core competency at your company—and it should be—the answers to these questions are vitally important to you. Did he observe major improprieties and say nothing, allowing them to continue? Or did she just ignore office supplies disappearing into employees' home offices? You are less concerned with the scale of unethical behavior than with the candidate's attitude toward improprieties. A series of probing, behavioral questions will help you identify those candidates whose ethical standards are below your own and/or your company's.

9

Questions About Core Competencies

Now that the generalities have been covered—pesky things such as motivation and the applicant's basic on-the-job attitude—it becomes important to glean even more particular information about a candidate's past performance.

Q: *Tell me about the last time you:*

- ◄ Made a mistake.
- ◄ Made a good decision.
- ◄ Made a poor decision.
- ◄ Fired someone.
- ◄ Hired someone.
- ◄ Were fired or laid off.
- ◄ Were asked to resign.
- ◄ Were denied a promotion.
- ◄ Delegated an important assignment.
- ◄ Led a team.

- ◄ Rallied your team.

- ◄ Motivated a troubled employee.

- ◄ Successfully completed a complex project.

- ◄ Learned a new skill.

- ◄ Developed a new expertise.

- ◄ Failed to complete a project on time.

- ◄ Found a unique solution to a problem.

- ◄ Found a creative solution to a problem.

- ◄ Found a cost-effective solution to a problem.

- ◄ Aimed too high.

- ◄ Aimed too low.

- ◄ Made (or lost) a great sale.

- ◄ Saved the company money.

- ◄ Cost the company money.

- ◄ Went over budget.

- ◄ Exceeded your own expectations.

- ◄ Exceeded your boss's expectations.

- ◄ Fell short of your boss's expectations.

- ◄ Had to think on your feet.

- ◄ Had to make an unpopular decision.

- ◄ Had to implement an unpopular decision.

- ◄ Dealt with a difficult boss.

- ◄ Dealt with a difficult customer.

- ◄ Dealt with a difficult coworker.

- ◄ Dealt with a difficult subordinate.

QUESTIONS ABOUT CORE COMPETENCIES

◄　Were frustrated at work.

◄　Were angry at work.

◄　Were stressed at work.

◄　Delivered a speech or major presentation.

◄　Questioned your boss's decision.

◄　Convinced your boss to change a decision.

◄　Went over your boss's head.

◄　Lost a battle but won the war.

What do you want to hear?

As I briefly discussed in Chapter 3, these are examples of competency-based interview questions. What are you trying to discover? According to Robin Kessler's *Competency-Based Interviews,* there are three general groups of competencies: those dealing with people, with business, and with self-management.

Competencies dealing with people include:

◄　Establishing focus.

◄　Providing motivational support.

◄　Fostering teamwork.

◄　Empowering others.

◄　Managing change.

◄　Developing others.

◄　Managing performance.

◄　Attention to communication.

◄　Oral communication.

◄　Written communication.

◄　Persuasive communication.

- ◄ Interpersonal awareness.
- ◄ Influencing others.
- ◄ Building collaborative relationships.
- ◄ Customer orientation.

Competencies dealing with business include:

- ◄ Diagnostic information gathering.
- ◄ Analytical thinking.
- ◄ Forward thinking.
- ◄ Conceptual thinking.
- ◄ Strategic thinking.
- ◄ Technical expertise.
- ◄ Initiative.
- ◄ Entrepreneurial orientation.
- ◄ Fostering innovation.
- ◄ Results orientation.
- ◄ Thoroughness.
- ◄ Decisiveness.

Finally, self-management competencies include:

- ◄ Self-confidence.
- ◄ Stress management.
- ◄ Personal credibility.
- ◄ Flexibility.

All questions are "open-ended," like "Tell me about yourself," thus encouraging the candidate to talk but clearly requiring focused, specific answers. Follow-up questions should be based on what the candidate answers initially: *"Okay, I understand how the lack of divisional coordination led to the budget shortfall. And you have clearly taken responsibility for your part in the miscommunication. But what did you do to change procedures to ensure it didn't happen again? And, by the way, did it happen again?"*

Just keep probing and asking for more specifics and examples: Who said what? Who did what? What were the results? What would you do differently now? What do you need to change to do better in the future? What *have* you changed?

The more detailed and clear-cut the job description you are working with, the more likely you have already identified the particular competencies required to succeed at it…and the more your questions should focus on those specific requirements.

 Thumbs up

A *specific* answer to a *specific* question, the more detailed the better.

An answer to any of the above questions that has a beginning, middle, and end, much like a good story: Here's what happened, here's what I did, here's what I learned. Problem. Action. Result.

Some of the questions *require* job-related answers; others may allow for examples chosen from outside activities, perhaps volunteer work or an aspect of one's personal life. A savvy candidate will mix and match stories and examples to convince you he is well-rounded and actually has a life after work.

A candidate who takes appropriate credit for an accomplishment (reducing costs, increasing revenues, a creative solution, a tough sale) but is fair and honest enough to put his own contribution within the context of what his team/organization/boss/assistants did.

A candidate who has been around long enough to make good *and* bad decisions, good *and* bad hires, good and bad *choices*. The breadth of a candidate's exposure to the basic tenets of business is more important to *me*, anyway, than the extent of her experience.

 Thumbs down

That "hard-working, self-starting, high-energy" Mr. Generalization who can't furnish you with any actual examples, no matter how many questions you toss him.

A candidate with years of experience in the same job who seems to have enjoyed little exposure to the normal day-to-day vagaries of the world. He hired someone once; they were fine. Never fired anyone. Can't remember the last time he actually had to make a major decision.

A candidate who was seemingly CEO/COO/CFO/creative star/sales guru—all at the same time. Even if you have a prodigy in your office, she should be savvy enough not to take credit for every success her company achieved in the last decade (especially if she's only been there three years).

Q: *What do you do when you're having trouble...*

◄ Solving a problem?

◄ With a subordinate?

◄ With a boss?

◄ With your job?

Q: *What do you do when...*

- ◄ Things are slow?

- ◄ Things are hectic?

- ◄ You're burned out?

- ◄ You have multiple priorities (family/work/school)?

What do you want to hear?

These questions are further attempts to home in on how each candidate really thinks and acts. Keep asking for specifics and examples. You may well have asked similar questions 10 or 30 minutes prior, so this gives you a chance to approach the same issue from a different direction. The style of question framed along the lines of "What do you do when...?" is very different from "Do you have problem with. . .?"

Q: *What are the skills you most need to acquire or develop to advance your career?*

What do you want to hear?

A successful candidate should be developing a skill in line with the job you have open. Otherwise why is he telling you about it? Needless to say, it probably shouldn't be a skill *required* for that position.

Q: *What do your supervisors tend to criticize most about your performance?*

What do you want to hear?

This is another way to frame a series of questions you've probably already asked: What's your greatest weakness? What was your greatest failure? What would your supervisor say about you?

By asking what amounts to the same question three or four different ways, it gives you a better chance to identify inconsistencies a candidate might well reveal—the second or third time around.

 Thumbs up

Because I assume you're going to be checking the candidate's references—and contacting his current supervisor after you've made the job offer—an answer that agrees with what the supervisor tells you should be expected. (And you may be able to use the candidate's answer to get a little more information from his ex-boss than he or she might have been willing to tell you otherwise.)

A candidate smart enough to discuss an evaluation from an earlier job, switching quickly to talk about what she did about it, and claiming that her current supervisor would, therefore, not consider it a problem any longer. The way to get around this elegant subterfuge is to follow up with a more specific question: "Was there anything your *current* supervisor criticized you for in your most recent performance evaluation?" "What specific areas did your current supervisor's last evaluation indicate you needed to work on?"

Whatever the answer, if the candidate cites concrete actions he or she is taking to change that behavior, I'd consider it a plus.

 Thumbs down

A candidate who cites a personal quality that might hamper his job performance, such as procrastination, laziness, lack of concentration, a hot temper, or tardiness.

A candidate who claims never to have received a poor evaluation. Although not necessarily untrue—there are companies and bosses that fail to do systematic evaluations or fail to take them very seriously—that answer won't give you the information you want. So consider a follow-up question, such as: "Tell me about the last time your boss criticized you. What for? What was your response? What have you done to fix/solve/change what he criticized?"

I would find it highly suspect for any candidate to claim she has *never* been called on the carpet for *anything*.

Q: *Did you inaugurate new procedures (systems, policies, etc.) in your previous position? Tell me about them.*

What do you want to hear?

Details about the specific, quantifiable results that were achieved or a good reason why his brilliant ideas (explained in detail, of course) were not implemented. You don't have to be a divisional president or department head to answer this question. An administrative assistant may have instituted a new filing system or improved a mundane task, like keeping the boss's calendar. You're looking for examples that will illustrate a candidate's initiative, creativity, and dedication to the organization and its success.

Again, a good answer should include facts and figures—the changes or improvements the candidate was responsible for making and how they helped the company increase profits, save money, or improve productivity.

What if she had some good ideas but circumstances didn't allow her company to take advantage of them? Here's a perfectly acceptable answer:

"Sure, we could have expanded our product line, perhaps even doubled it, to take advantage of our superior distribution. But we just didn't have the capital and couldn't get the financing."

Variations

- ◄ Tell me about the last time you did more than your boss expected.

- ◄ Give me an example of your industriousness.

- ◄ Whose job is it to come up with new ideas?

- ◄ Explain the difference between a problem and an opportunity.

- ◄ When did you last request additional responsibility?

- ◄ Give me an example when you "did more with less."

- ◄ Have you ever done something that needed to be done even though it wasn't part of your job description?

- ◄ What did you do at your last job that wasn't expected of you?

Q: Have you been in charge of budgeting, approving expenses, and monitoring departmental progress against financial goals? Are you qualified in this area?

What do you want to hear?

Financial responsibility signals an employer's faith in someone. Depending on the position you're trying to fill, this may well be a requirement, and the candidate's answer to this single question may be the greatest predictor of his or her fate.

If a candidate hasn't had many—or any—fiscal duties, he should admit it, though nothing is stopping him from creatively framing his reply:

"Well, I've never actually run a department, but I've had to set and meet budgetary goals for several projects I've worked on. In fact, I did this so often that I took a class to learn how to set up and use Microsoft Excel spreadsheets and Quickbooks."

If she has had broader responsibilities, you should expect her to talk about her approval authority. What is the largest expenditure she could sign off on? A solid candidate will let you know, in round numbers, the income and expenses of the departments she has supervised.

If the candidate claims to be very qualified, making her a viable contender for the position, here's a good, broad follow-up question: "What are the most common obstacles you've faced when completing assignments or projects on time and on budget? Give me one or two examples and how you dealt with them."

Q: Have you ever fired anyone? Why?

What do you want to hear?

You and the candidate both know firing someone is never pleasant. She should say so, and then provide a brief "sanitized" version of the events. You should expect a modicum of sympathy for the person (people) who got the axe, an understanding that sometimes people have to be fired, and a readiness to do it appropriately, professionally, and compassionately, when required. A reasonable answer may be:

"Yes, I fired someone who continually fell short of his productivity goals. His shortcomings were documented and discussed with him over a period of months. But in that time he failed to show any real improvement. I had no choice. As a supervisor, I want everyone in my department to work out. Let's face it, though. Not everyone is equally dedicated to his or her job."

If a candidate hasn't ever actually fired anyone, you should expect a response like this:

"I've never actually fired anyone myself, but it was the policy at my company that no hirings or firings should be unilateral. I was asked on two occasions to give my opinion about someone else's performance. It's never easy to be honest about a coworker's shortcomings. But I felt I had to do what was best for the department and fair to everyone else in it."

Q: Have you ever hired anyone? Why did you choose them?

What do you want to hear?

If the candidate has hired one or more people during his or her career, a good answer might go something like this:

"Yes, I have hired people. I have also decided whether some internal applicants were right for jobs in my department. The first time I hired someone, I just went down a checklist of required skills and experience. Since then, I've learned that some candidates who became excellent workers didn't necessarily have every qualification on that checklist. They more than make up for what they lacked in the beginning with enthusiasm and a willingness to work with others."

What if he never hired anyone? You should hope he appreciates you are trying to evaluate his management potential as well as his people skills and expect an answer like this:

"Not really. But on several occasions I was asked to speak to prospective applicants and offer my opinion to management. Of course, in those cases, I was trying to determine if that person would be a team player and if he or she would get along with the other people in the department."

Q: See that picture frame on the wall? Sell it to me.

Or the pen, the desk, the paperweight, whatever. I'm not sure I particularly like this question—although it isn't a horrible one to ask entry-level sales candidates.

What do you want to hear?

One of the major characteristics of a truly good salesperson is his or her ability to ask questions and listen to the answers (kind of like a really good interviewer). So a good sales candidate will begin by asking a series of questions about the object and about your particular needs.

An old friend of mine, a sales superstar, once told me that if he asked enough questions, and asked enough of the *right* questions, sooner or later every prospect would tell him exactly what he needed to say to get the sale.

Obviously, the ultimate test of a sales candidate is whether he or she is really capable of selling that object to you. I suspect if you're a sales manager hiring salespeople, you have your own little tests to ascertain whether a candidate has what it takes.

What about the candidate who will have nothing to do with sales? This may still be a viable question if only to see how he reacts under pressure. The less sales-oriented a candidate is, the more this question will bother him, making it a reasonable way to put him into a pressure cooker and see if he boils.

Variations

- ◄ Tell me about the last time you turned a "no" into a "yes."
- ◄ What sales courses have you taken?
- ◄ What sales seminars have you attended?
- ◄ Do you believe in question-based selling? Why or why not?

- ◄   What do your consider your sales style?
- ◄   How do you see yourself fitting into our sales function?

Get the information you need

I could make a strong case that you need only ask one question, something like "Explain in detail the last task or project you undertook," in order to learn a tremendous amount about any candidate. The secret is how you follow up after the initial answer. If you ask enough probing questions, you will gain an extremely detailed picture of how the candidate thinks, how he leads and motivates, his problem-solving and analytical skills, his good sense (based on the example he chooses and the details he reveals), his concept of success (based on the results achieved…or not), and much, much more.

The following examples are two sets of follow-up questions, not in any order and not exhaustive. The first group is a serviceable template to utilize after a candidate's initial response to the above question:

- ◄   Who was in charge of the project?
- ◄   To whom did you report?
- ◄   Why do you think you were chosen for this task?
- ◄   Were you qualified to participate in this task?
- ◄   Were you qualified to run this project?
- ◄   Who else was involved?
- ◄   What was your plan?
- ◄   Explain in detail the role of each person involved.
- ◄   What was management's reaction to your plan?
- ◄   What was management's reaction to your result?

- What skills were required to fulfill your plan?
- Were you provided with sufficient input?
- Were you provided with the correct input?
- Were you given a sufficient budget?
- Were you given sufficient time?
- What constraints did you suffer from?
- Did you request anything that was denied?
- What were the reasons for the denial?
- Did you agree with them?
- What happened that you did not anticipate?
- Why didn't you anticipate that?
- Were there resources you needed that weren't available?
- How did you make up for them?
- Were there people needed that weren't available?
- How did you function without them?
- What changes did lack of people or resources require you to make?
- How did you dole out assignments?
- What conflicts arose?
- How did you deal with them?
- Were there mistakes you missed?
- Were there mistakes you overlooked?
- Why did you overlook them?
- Tell me about some major decisions you had to make.
- Tell me about decisions made with which you did not agree.

◄ Tell me about decisions you fought for and lost.

◄ Tell me about decisions you fought for and won.

◄ Give me some examples of your leadership role.

◄ Were there previous attempts to accomplish this goal?

◄ Why and how did they fail?

◄ How did you change your approach based on these previous attempts?

◄ What do you think you *should* have done differently?

◄ What do you think you *could* have done differently?

◄ What did you have to learn to accomplish this task?

◄ What part of the task did you enjoy most?

◄ What part of the task did you enjoy least?

◄ How did you specifically motivate others?

◄ How did you specifically influence others?

◄ Detail the results achieved.

◄ What did this experience teach you?

◄ How did this experience change you?

The second group consists of simpler probing questions that can be used after virtually any answer to any question:

◄ What did you do?

◄ Why did you do that?

◄ Why didn't you do that?

◄ What did you say?

◄ How did he or she react?

◄ What was his or her answer?

◄ What happened then?

◄ How did you prepare for that?

◄ How did you handle that?

◄ How did you react to that?

◄ When did you learn that?

◄ Did you agree with that decision?

◄ What did you think would happen?

◄ Were you right?

◄ What did you do then?

◄ What did you learn from that?

Is a fuller picture of that candidate beginning to emerge? Is there a real, live, breathing person in front of you now, rather than the cipher that shook your hand? Good. It's working.

In the next chapter, we'll continue to home in on the candidate's most recent experience.

10

QUESTIONS ABOUT THE MOST RECENT JOB

Whether the candidate before you has been working for 20 years or 20 days, it is human nature to focus on the most recent job even if it boasted the shortest tenure or even if a previous job was for years and the current one lasted just months. Why? Because you want to know what the candidate can do for you—right now—and the most current job offers the best available proof.

Q: Why are you thinking of leaving your current job?

What do you want to hear?

Obviously, no one wants to leave a job with which they are completely content (although some people routinely interview to keep in practice). But the last thing you want is a candidate who enthusiastically highlights the negative aspects of his current job or, worse, speaks ill of his current employer. It may not be fair to the interviewee, who may well be giving you just the negative "tip of the iceberg" of the Job from Hell, but many of you will assume that, if hired, the candidate will soon be characterizing you and your company in the same disparaging terms.

So a candidate should handle her discontent (if that's what led her here) very gingerly. The less contented she is, the more careful she should be when talking about it. Here's a good answer:

"There is a great deal I enjoy about my current job. But my potential for growth in this area is limited at Closely Held, Inc., because of the size of the company and the fact that expansion is not a part of its current strategic plan."

 Thumbs up

Unless they have been fired or laid off, viable candidates should make it clear that they are sitting in front of you only because they seek more responsibility, a bigger challenge, or better opportunities for growth (even more money), *not* because they are desperate to put some distance between themselves and their current job situation.

Emphasizing a desire to move "up," not just "out," and the avoidance of any personal and/or negative comments about coworkers, supervisors, or the current company's policies are also red flags.

 Thumbs down

The introduction of any negative, no matter how horrible the current job situation. (In fact, the more obviously horrible his job, the more points a candidate should score in your eyes for creating an impression of relative contentment.)

A willingness to make a lateral move or even take a demotion just to leave the current company. Unless the candidate is moving into an entirely new area or field, such a willingness to move out rather than up would concern me. What is he or she hiding? Is this just a last-ditch effort to get out before he's shoved out? And what does such a willingness say about his ability to tough it out until the right situation comes along? Is your company just a calmer sea in which he can tread water until the right freighter passes by?

Variations

◄ What's hindering your progress at your present firm?

◄ Is this the first time you've thought about leaving? What made you stay before?

◄ If the situation is so bleak, why haven't you already given notice?

Q: *Where does your boss think you are now?*

What do you want to hear?

It's rare to hear something like, "He thinks I'm interviewing with you so I can leave that hellhole behind and, by the way, he'll be calling you tomorrow to find a job himself." If they are still employed, you should expect candidates to be seeing you during their lunch hours, after work, or on a personal or vacation day. I personally don't like to hear that a candidate has taken a sick day to talk with me. It's a white lie, but a lie nonetheless.

If the candidate has been laid off, fired, or already given notice, you should have elicited that information earlier in the interview.

Thumbs up

◄ The truth, whatever it is.

◄ A candidate who demonstrates his or her responsibility to a current job by scheduling a breakfast interview or one during a lunch hour or after hours. After all, until he leaves, he is still being paid by his current company for a fair day's work.

 Thumbs down

◄ A candidate who has blatantly lied or indicates through body language that the question makes him uncomfortable (implying that he *did* lie).

◄ A candidate who demonstrates little or no loyalty to the company that's still paying his bills, whether that organization is enlightened or despotic.

Q: Are you still employed at the last firm listed on your resume?

What do you want to hear?

You probably know the adage that it's always easier to find a job when you already have one. It's still true, because many interviewers believe that an employed person is somehow better than an unemployed one, even if the latter is more qualified. Being laid off is perceived by many interviewers as a sign of weakness, despite the millions who have recently suffered that fate. I even heard one experienced executive recruiter say, "Oh, if she was laid off, there must be something wrong with her.

Companies don't ever let really good employees go!" Would that it were true!

But the fact is that layoffs still occur regularly. And many hard-working, loyal individuals who contributed greatly to their companies—and could be significant assets to yours—have to admit they've been laid off. I am firmly convinced there should be no shame in this status and a laid-off candidate should be given the same consideration as anyone else. And I suggest you do likewise.

What if they were fired? Expect them to come clean quickly, and then smoothly turn this potential negative into a positive.

 Thumbs up

A candidate who talks less about why she was terminated and more about what she learned from the experience.

If she was laid off, or, as the British quaintly say, "made redundant," you shouldn't expect her to apologize. You might like to hear something like, "Yes, I was one of 160 people laid off when sales took a slide."

(The above statement is an easy way out—presuming she was not a member of the sales department or, worse, responsible for a significant portion of the slide!)

 Thumbs down

As always, the introduction of any negative: *"Yes, I was fired because I'm not as young as I used to be. Wait until they see what my old lawyer has to say about age discrimination. I'll make them pay through the nose!"*

Firing for cause, especially if the individual refuses to admit responsibility or detail steps taken to correct the problem. Most interviewers get understandably nervous hiring someone who was fired for stealing, drinking on the job, hitting his boss, or some equally charming offense.

Q: Describe the way your department is organized. What is the title of the person to whom you report? What are his or her exact responsibilities?

What do you want to hear?

If someone has been vastly exaggerating the duties and responsibilities of his current position, this question will send him spiraling to a crash landing.

It should clarify what he really does—how can *he* be doing "X" if he now declares that's his *boss's* main function? And it sets up a series of follow-up questions, which may include a request to draw an organizational chart of his department.

Many of you will use such a response as the basis for immediate rejection. I can't argue that you shouldn't.

 Thumbs up

◄ Duties and responsibilities that match those claimed on the candidate's resume.

◄ Duties and responsibilities commensurate with the job at hand.

◄ An answer that makes sense given the candidate's answers to previous questions about work experience. The more detailed these answers—and the more you've probed to get them—the easier it will be to catch any inconsistencies (at which point you'll want to return to those previous answers and ask why the current one doesn't seem to mesh with them).

◄ A clearly presented explanation of how her department, division, or company is set up, which is consistent with her resume and implies that she has really done what she said she did. You will, of course, take detailed notes and check these claims when you call her supervisor for a reference, won't you?

 Thumbs down

◄ A hazy, vague explanation that indicates the candidate may be making it all up as he goes along.

◄ Glaring inconsistencies with the resume or previous answers.

◄ Failure to include a key responsibility or job duty that was previously proclaimed, especially if it's one that is important to you.

◄ An organizational plan that doesn't make sense to you. The more experience you have at different companies, the more likely you will have been exposed to different structures and management styles, and the more confident you will feel that a structure that seems top heavy or one that gives lower-level staff members an extraordinary amount of freedom just doesn't feel right. Use your own experience to craft a series of questions that will paint a fast-talking candidate into a corner.

Q: Tell me about a typical day at your current (last) job. How much time do you spend on the phone? In meetings? Reading and responded to emails? In one-on-one chats? Working by yourself? Working with your team (or others)?

What do you want to hear?

Again, you're looking for the detail that will support some of the earlier general statements the candidate has made about responsibilities, duties, even favorite aspects of the job, or that will show those statements were disingenuous or somewhat excessive.

Variations

◄ On a typical day, tell me what you do in the first and last hour at work. When do you arrive and leave?

◄ Tell me what specific responsibilities you currently delegate. Are you delegating too many or too few tasks? Why? What's stopping you from changing it?

◄ How many hours per week do you have to work to fulfill your responsibilities?

◄ What's the most important part of your current job to you? To your firm?

Q: How long have you been looking for a job?

What do you want to hear?

Unless someone has been fired or laid off, a candidate should always answer that he has just started looking. Why? Because rightly or wrongly, many interviewers presume that the longer someone's been out there, the less desirable he is to hire. Needless to say, if you have some way of finding out that the candidate in front of you has been looking for a while (perhaps she was recommended by a recruiter who knows her history), she should be prepared to explain why she hasn't received or accepted any offers.

Is this a prejudice you should buy into? If someone's been looking for a month or two or three, is she inherently less desirable than a newly minted *ex*-employee? It's unrealistic to expect that everyone who wants a job can find one right away. It's even less realistic not to assume that the most qualified candidates might be picky and simply be ensuring a proper fit with the right company before diving back into the corporate seas.

Variations

◄   How's your job search coming?

◄   How optimistic are you about getting a job?

Q: *What other companies have you interviewed with?*

What do you want to hear?

This is a not-so-veiled way to see if the candidate is being consistent. If the other companies with which he has interviewed are in entirely different industries (or states!), or if the jobs he is pursuing bear no relation to your opening, how serious a candidate can he be? The more disparate the companies, the more you should question the candidate's assurances that you are the end-all and be-all of his career quest.

Variations

◄   Have you interviewed with any of our competitors?

◄   Why haven't you gotten interviews with more companies?

◄   Why have you interviewed with so many companies?

◄   Why did you interview with *them*?

◄   What specific positions did you apply for at each company?

Q: *Why haven't you received any offers so far?*

What do you want to hear?

Presuming the answer to the previous question was *not* "Oh, you're my first interview," you should expect a candidate to claim that she is just as choosy about finding the right job as you are about hiring the right candidate. If she has already fielded an offer or two, you might expect to hear:

"I have had an offer, but the situation was not right for me. I'm especially glad that I didn't accept it, because I now have a shot at landing this position."

This is one of those nice generalizations that can cover up a bucket of sins, but you certainly don't have to accept such an answer at face value. Your next logical question may be:

Q: *Who made you an offer? For what type of position? At what salary?*

What do you want to hear?

If the candidate has already lied, you're about to make her wish she hadn't! For one thing, you probably know a great deal about your competitors and which positions they're trying to fill. So if the candidate proffers information you know to be inaccurate, you can be pretty sure there's a secret to uncover and should move ahead with a series of pointed follow-up questions.

Again, some interviewers will take any admission of lying in these circumstances as a voluntary offer by the candidate to end the interview!

Q: Tell me about the last time you turned down a job or promotion and regretted your decision. Why did you regret it? What did it teach you?

What do you want to hear?

Asking for a detailed description of the job she turned down may give you some very pertinent information. You will often find that the other job is completely different than the one she's seeking with your company. Shouldn't this be a red flag? After all, if the job for which she's currently interviewing is "perfect"—as she's proclaimed three or four times already—why would she be interested in a very different job at the other company?

Q: If you don't leave your current job, what will happen there? How far do you expect to advance?

What do you want to hear?

Even if the candidate would rather hawk peanuts on the street than stay another month at ABC Widget, he should seek to convince you that he is the type of employee who is capable of making the most of any situation, even an employment situation he's characterized as less than desirable. He could say:

"Naturally I'm interested in this job and have been thinking about leaving ABC. However, my supervisors think highly of me, and I expect that one day other opportunities will open up for me at the company. I'm one of ABC's top salespeople. I have seen other people performing at similar levels advance to management positions. That's what I'm looking for right now."

Thumbs up

◄ A candidate who claims she will still advance and be given more responsibility, but perhaps at too slow a pace or without adequate compensation.

◄ A situation in which the company, through little or no fault of the candidate's, will clearly not be able to keep or pay its top people what they're worth, perhaps due to a pending merger, bankruptcy, cash flow problems, or loss of a key customer or product. Clearly, the candidate's reason for leaving is obvious and justifiable and his future there is dim.

 Thumbs down

◄ "Well, I doubt I'll last the week. Old Scrawnynose will probably fire me right after lunch."

◄ An answer that indicates problems at the company for which the candidate must bear some responsibility: "Well, sales are down 10 percent across the board but my territory is down 32 percent. It's not my fault so many stores went out of business!"

Q: If you're so happy at your current job, why are you leaving? Will they be surprised?

What do you want to hear?

I think this is a very difficult question for many interviewees to answer. The more positive they have attempted to be (following all that advice from authors prepping *them*) the smaller the corner they've seemingly painted themselves into.

Some candidates know full well their current company will go out of business at any second. Others dread spending another day under a tyrannical boss or need to get out of a job that simply never lived up to its billing. Of course, they've tried to "paper over" any of these negatives. So *now* what do they say?

A winning candidate will take a deep breath and calmly reassure you that she's made the decision to move toward more responsibility, more knowledge, and the wonderful opportunity available at your company.

What about the "Will they be surprised?" follow-up? I think either answer puts the candidate in a box. If they *won't* be surprised, then all of his other answers better confirm that he simply can't advance, can't get the raises he deserves, is truly working for a company on the verge of a nervous breakdown, or something similar. In other words, the situation truly should be wrong for this candidate, and if his supervisor was called (and you will call somewhere along the line), he or she would confirm that the candidate is a winner but it's the wrong time, place, boss, company, whatever.

If they *will* be surprised, then it's unlikely the situation itself is untenable (unless the candidate has, admirably, suffered in complete silence for lo these many months).

Variations

◄ What have you had to change about yourself/your skills/your philosophy/your duties to adapt to changes at your current firm?

◄ What would have to change at your current job to make it tenable?

◄ What aspects of your current job were different than you expected when you took it?

Q: If you have complaints about your current job/boss/ company, and they think so highly of you, why haven't you brought your concerns to their attention?

What do you want to hear?

Again, you are essentially taking the candidate who has attempted to remain highly positive throughout the interview and "hoisting him by his own petard."

This is a dead-end for many candidates, except for those smart enough to stay positive despite your best efforts to corner them. A winning answer might be like the following:

"Grin & Bear It is aware of my desire to move up. But the company is still small. There's really not much they can do about it. The management team is terrific. There's no need right now to add to it, and they are aware of some of the problems this creates in keeping good performers. It's something they openly talk about."

Variations

◄ If you could make one comment or suggestion to your current boss, what would it be? Did you do anything of the sort? Why or why not?

◄ If you could eliminate one duty/responsibility from your current job, what would it be and why?

Q: How would your coworkers describe you?

What do you want to hear?

Of course, you would expect that they would describe the candidate as an easygoing person who is a good team player.

Be careful of overly broad descriptions that could be extracted whole from the *Scout Handbook*. Simply ask for a job-related experience to illustrate each supposed trait.

 Thumbs up

Presuming you have your own mental picture of your ideal candidate—and a list of attributes you consider essential—your list and the candidate's should be a good match.

 Thumbs down

◄ A description that bears little resemblance to the characteristics and skills required for the job at hand.

◄ The inability to cite specific examples to back up his claims.

Variations

◄ What five adjectives would your last supervisor use to describe you?

◄ How effectively did your supervisor conduct appraisals?

◄ How did you do on your last performance appraisal?

◄ What were the key strengths and weaknesses mentioned by your supervisor?

◄ How did your last supervisor get the best performance out of you?

◄ What did you say and do the last time you were right and your boss was wrong?

Q: *Give me specific examples of what you did at your current (last) job to increase revenues, reduce costs, be more efficient, or something similar.*

What do you want to hear?

This ties into the earlier questions you asked about budgetary responsibility and how the candidate's current department is organized. It's a good idea after asking the first question or two to ask some different questions, *then* return to the subject later. Many candidates, having successfully navigated the shoals of the earlier questions, may be caught in an exaggeration when you return to the question later on rather than following up immediately.

Q: *What do you feel an employer owes an employee?*

What do you want to hear?

A smart candidate will avoid getting into a dissertation on the employer's moral or, worse, legal responsibility to employees. Instead, she will try to refocus your attention on her positive outlook. Because detail breeds follow-up questions, this candidate may attempt very brief answers. By continuing to probe, you can, of course, continue to apply the pressure when you get an answer like this:

"I think an employer owes its employees opportunity. In my next position, I look forward to the opportunity to run projects profitably."

It's up to you how much you care to probe, and it may well be a function of your particular company. For example, it may be important to you to clarify a candidate's feelings about the information an employer should share with employees or the size of the raise pool. But a good candidate will be able to joust with you:

"I hope that my employer will be respectful of me as an employee and of any agreements we may negotiate in the course of business. However, I know that there are times when organizations face tough decisions that may require confidentiality and affect employees. That's business."

Q: The successful candidate for this position will be working with some highly trained individuals who have been with the company for a long time. How will you mesh with them?

What do you want to hear?

A successful candidate should convince you of her eagerness, as the new kid on the block, to learn from her future coworkers. You would expect her to avoid raising any doubts about how they might react to her and to use the opportunity you have given her to humbly chat about how much she needs to learn…even if, in her heart of hearts, she thinks they're probably all a bunch of old fogies and can't wait to get on board and shape them up. This question could be used to assess a candidate's approach toward teamwork, along with some of the following:

Variations

◄ Tell me about the last team you worked with or led.

◄ Is a team approach always the most efficient one?

◄ Tell me about a project that required you to deal with a variety of different people who did not report to you.

◄ Tell me about the last team you led and assess each individual's contribution to the end result.

Q: *Your supervisor tells you do to something in a way you know is dead wrong. What do you do?*

What do you want to hear?

This is a tough question. A careful interviewee may try to slide by:

"In a situation like this, even the best employee runs the risk of seeming insubordinate. I would pose my alternative to my supervisor in the most deferential way possible. If he insisted that I was wrong, I guess I'd have to do it his way."

This answer may be fine if you're hiring a subordinate and work for a company that lives and dies by the chain of command. If you're seeking hot-blooded self-starters, this answer could doom an otherwise qualified candidate.

Q: *If you were unfairly criticized by your supervisor, what would you do?*

What do you want to hear?

All of us can think back to a time when pressure at work led to mistakes. Maybe you took more than your fair share of the blame. Perhaps you were caught in circumstances beyond your control. In any event, your boss blamed you.

The candidate undoubtedly has gone through a similar situation and should craft an answer that refers to a specific experience. If he's smart, it won't be the most vulnerable or perilous moment of his career. An expected answer may come out like this:

"In the course of my career there have been a few times when problems have come up and I have been held accountable for mistakes I did not feel I had caused. But a problem is a problem no matter who creates it, and you certainly don't have to create the problem to solve it. The most important thing is to deal with it.

"On those occasions when the issue has been significant enough, I have explained my point of view to my supervisor later—after the situation has been resolved and the atmosphere has calmed."

Q: Would you like to have your boss's job? Why or why not?

What do you want to hear?

No matter how someone answers this question, you should learn a lot about her. It's an indirect way of finding out whether she wants to be promoted.

Let's start with the first part of the question: A "yes" answer identifies a candidate who is ambitious and interested in career advancement. A "no" indicates doubts or reservations, at least about the job in question.

In the second part of the question, things get sticky for some candidates who have sailed through the earlier stages of the interview. For instance, if it's clear that someone is interested in promotion and the position he is applying for doesn't offer a path to a higher level, then you may well conclude that he'll be disappointed. On the other hand, if you're in a highly competitive organization, you may reject out of hand a candidate who expresses reservations about career advancement.

 Thumbs up

Even if you've caught someone totally off guard with this question, the answer better be positive and should mesh with your company's culture. It can be as simple as the following examples:

175

"In time, I would love to have my boss's job. I'm particularly interested in the vendor relationships and sales promotion sides of buying."

"I am very interested in career advancement, but my current boss's responsibilities are heavily weighted toward managing department production. In time, I hope to move into a position with primary responsibility for design quality."

"I would be open to taking on additional responsibilities, but I like the autonomy of a sales position, and I find it rewarding to work directly with clients. My boss is mainly responsible for supervising the department and its personnel. In such a position, I would miss the client contact."

Q: *Please tell me a joke.*

Please don't ask.

This is the only example I am going to include of questions that, for lack of a better term, are stupid. I personally don't care what kind of tree a candidate thinks he is, what animal represents her management style, or what his zodiacal sign means, and neither should you. But, of course, some of you do.

A smart candidate will treat any such question—or a suggestion like "Tell me a joke"—as the unwelcome diversion that it is and find a way to bring the conversation back to the particulars he knows he needs to emphasize and the traits and skills you really do want to hear about.

And she can always craft an answer that discusses how a sense of humor is an important attribute when diffusing a volatile situation, along with a pertinent example.

11

QUESTIONS FOR MANAGERS AND EXECUTIVES

If you're hiring at the executive level, most of the previous questions in this book are just as pertinent as if you were hiring an entry-level clerk (although you would expect a different level of answer!). This chapter features questions specifically for that potential CFO, CIO, or executive vice president.

Q: Describe your management philosophy.

What do you want to hear?

Someone who can demonstrate a desire and ability to delegate, teach, and distribute work—and credit—fairly (unless, of course, you are an autocratic jerk and seek a mirror image). In general, you probably want neither a dictator nor a pushover. A successful candidate should convey that she has the ability to succeed should opportunity present itself.

177

But she should avoid giving the impression that she's a fire-breathing workaholic ready to succeed no matter what (or who) the cost.

 Thumbs up

"More than anything else, I think that management is getting things done through other people. The manager's job is to provide the resources and environment in which people can work effectively. I try to do this by creating teams, judging people solely on the basis of their performance, distributing work fairly, and empowering workers, to the extent possible, to make their own decisions. I've found that this breeds loyalty and inspires hard work."

 Thumbs down

One of these answers, all of which I've actually heard during interviews:

- ◄ "I try to get people to like me so they'll really work hard for me."

- ◄ "I guess you could say I'm a real people-person."

- ◄ "I just kind of let things happen and deal with problems as they develop."

- ◄ "I don't know."

Variations

- ◄ Explain to me your overall approach to this position.

Is he a gunslinger ready to clean up Dodge City? A wallflower willing to watch while everyone else joins the dance? Or a candidate smart enough to assess the lay of the land before rushing headlong into a minefield?

Q: What did you do the last time someone approached you with a problem (complaint, fear, mistake)?

What do you want to hear?

Does the paragon who so carefully answered the previous question take a little too long to answer this one? If so, maybe detailing his management philosophy isn't hard...because he's never really had much management *experience*.

Is her answer consistent with the philosophy she just expressed? Did she handle the situation in the way you would want her to if she reported to you?

Q: Tell me the kind of example you set for your employees (coworkers, team members).

What do you want to hear?

You are giving her a chance to give you specific examples that prove she walks the management talk she just enumerated. Don't you want a manager who actually embodies the philosophy she proclaims and the behaviors she expects from her employees, team-members, and/or coworkers? Of course you do.

Q: What's the most difficult part of being a manager or executive?

Q: Tell me about the last situation in which you were directed to overhaul a problem unit/department/division/company. What were you confronted with, what did you do, and what kind of culture did you attempt to create?

Q: *How many people did you hire and fire?*

Q: *What goals did you establish?*

Q: *How long was your outlook, and what were the results?*

What do you want to hear?

Every one of these questions is designed to further expose a candidate's management philosophy and gauge his or her abilities to conceptualize on a general basis and implement on a specific one: to foster loyalty, unity, and shared goals; to create and produce under pressure; to stay within budget; and so on. You expect to hear very specific examples that detail the problems a candidate faced, the actions he or she took, and the results achieved.

Variations

◄ What kinds of decisions are difficult for you to make?

◄ How do you go about making a decision?

◄ How do you decide what tasks to delegate and to whom?

◄ Tell me about the last responsibility you delegated that went wrong.

◄ What was the worst decision you ever made?

◄ How much feedback do you want from your subordinates?

◄ Tell me about the last decision you made that your subordinates disagreed with.

◄ Tell me about the last decision you made that your boss disagreed with.

Pick a detail, either a positive or a negative, and keep probing. Feel free to borrow from the long list of probing questions at the end of Chapter 9.

Q: How do you deal with subordinates who are becoming part of the problem rather than part of the solution?

What do you want to hear?

This has been asked previously in other forms. You're trying to separate the real leaders from the "managers with a title" and ascertain whether this candidate's style will mesh with yours.

Q: What factors do you consider most important when you evaluate the performance of a team member or direct report?

What do you want to hear?

Candidates may identify those traits they want *their* bosses to consider, giving you a sense of how *they* want to be treated. You may uncover a candidate's tendency to undervalue employee performance appraisals. Or the candidate's assessments may strike you as shallow or off-the-mark.

Q: How do you "stay in the loop"?

What do you want to hear?

There are many ways to get the information you are seeking with this question. Here are some other possible questions:

◄ How many meetings do you schedule and/or attend per week? Per month?

◄ Do you believe in "management-by-walking-around"?

- ◄ Do you spend a lot of time in your subordinates' offices asking questions or do you prefer to wait for them to come to you with problems?

- ◄ Tell me about the last time you skipped a meeting? Why didn't you attend?

- ◄ What regular communications do you expect from your employees?

All of the above are much more specific than "Describe your management philosophy," a question an experienced interviewee can wiggle through with a couple of business-guru quotes. The more senior the candidate's current position—and the more executive the position for which he or she is applying—the more these types of questions should be asked. And the more important the answers to them will be.

Q: *Tell me about a project you had to undertake with inadequate input/planning/money/people.*

What do you want to hear?

A savvy candidate will have answered previous questions with glowing reports of raging success. Yet anyone who has been in business has inevitably found himself trying to make things happen when the deadline is too short, the money too tight, or the goal too ephemeral. How did he respond under *those* circumstances? What did he do to overcome these obstacles? And if she claims to have never been in that situation, has she really been tested? Are you looking to hire someone who can be successful when everything is in place but doesn't have any experience dealing with the inevitable day-to-day snafus?

Q: Tell me about the last time you had to accomplish a task or complete a project when the input you were given was ambiguous, conflicting, or just plain wrong?

What do you want to hear?

How ready are they to go to the Dark Side and trash all those incompetents that made that task so onerous? Again, it is likely that anyone in business for any length of time will find himself trying to complete a task with two departments giving him conflicting input, for a boss who isn't quite sure what he wants accomplished but knows he wants it *now*, or with incomplete, inadequate, or flat-out wrong input. Can she stay positive while answering this question?

Q: Tell me about the last time you had to work on a project you disliked or even hated.

What do you want to hear?

This is the most negative of the last three questions, all designed to elicit a candidate's acknowledgement that she hasn't lived in a perfect world and has adapted as required in order to reach successful outcomes. You are trying to uncover a candidate's tendency to dwell on the negative or simply wish it weren't always so hard. You are seeking someone with the guts to admit she has confronted far-from-perfect situations but has nevertheless always (or mostly always) found ways to prevail.

When asked to differentiate between a professional and an amateur, my short answer is always to note that a professional can produce *passable* (not perfect or even great) reports, presentations, solutions, ideas, and so on, no matter his or her physical, emotional, or mental state. Amateurs may produce excellent work when suitably motivated but find it difficult or impossible to even function when circumstances are more difficult.

Q: Tell me about the last time you had to convince your boss or upper management to do something they didn't want to do.

What do you want to hear?

You could learn a great deal from this answer, especially if you follow up with questions to elicit more details: Did the candidate originate the project or idea? Why didn't management want to go along? Were their reasons valid? What arguments did the candidate cite to make her case? Was she successful? Was the project successful? What was management's reaction? If she wasn't able to convince them, how did she handle the rejection?

Variations

◄ Tell me about the last time you had to convince your coworkers to do something they didn't want to do.

◄ Tell me about the last time you had to convince your team to do something they didn't want to do.

◄ Tell me about the last time you had to convince your employees to do something they actively resisted.

◄ Tell me about the last time you did a good job communicating to your boss, upper management, team, or coworkers. What did you do? What was the result?

◄ Tell me about the last time you did a poor job communicating to your boss, upper management, or coworkers. What did you do? What was the result? What have you done become a better communicator?

Q: Tell me about the last speech or presentation you gave.

What do you want to hear?

If communication is a core competency of the job at hand, it is imperative you seek to assess the candidate's oral and written communication skills. More important, you want concrete examples of reports and presentations she has prepared and a clear understanding of how she will utilize her purported skills working for you. Although few candidates will come to an interview with such samples, they should expect you to request them if they are still considered viable candidates. An inability to produce original reports that resulted in tangible results or affected management decisions should be considered a red flag.

You can use some of the following variations to further assess the candidate's skills at writing reports and giving presentations, but also his or her ability to actively listen and effectively communicate with bosses, team members, and subordinates.

Variations

◄ Have you ever led a seminar?

◄ Tell me about how you prefer to communicate to your boss, team members, coworkers and/or subordinates.

◄ Tell me about the last time you had to convince someone using your written communication skills.

◄ Tell me about the last time you had to convince someone using your oral communication skills.

◄ Do you have any examples of reports you've written or presentations you've given?

◄ How do you know you're "getting through" to someone?

◄ Tell me about the last time you failed to adequately communicate an important detail to a subordinate.

◄ Tell me about the last time you misunderstood a communication from your boss.

◄ Tell me about the last time your failure to listen resulted in a problem.

Q: *Tell me about your personal code of ethics.*

What do you want to hear?

No matter what their actual ethics or moral code, a candidate should clearly emphasize his or her honesty, loyalty, and integrity, all attributes any company should value and welcome. And if he or she is willing to do just about anything to get ahead and barely knows the difference between right and wrong? I wouldn't expect anyone to confess such a lack of integrity…or schedule an interview at my company.

Variations

◄ Tell me about the last time you did something inconsistent with your values or ethics.

◄ Have you ever had to "bend the rules" to do your job?

◄ Tell me about the last time you uncovered or learned about a coworker's unethical behavior. What did you do?

◄ What would you do if you learned this company was doing something you thought was wrong?

Q: *Would you lie for your company?*

What do you want to hear?

"Never have, never would. I value my own conscience too much to bend my principles."

Q: *A colleague told you she is looking for a job but asked you to keep her confidence. What would you say if your boss asked you point blank about it?*

What do you want to hear?

The candidate may not be a snitch and be able to keep a secret, but he or she must convince you that his or her loyalty to the company trumps loyalty to a colleague, subordinate, or friend. Can he or she think of any (equally hypothetical) way to protect that person's confidence without lying to the boss? Finding such a solution would certainly highlight their diplomatic skills.

Variations

◄   Would you lie to cover up a mistake or ethical violation by your boss (colleague, subordinate, team member)?

◄   When is it okay to break a confidence?

◄   When is it okay to reveal another's secret?

Companies protecting valuable patents, product recipes, and other corporate secrets are now assailed daily by computer hackers. A loss of confidential information to a competitor could be devastating. Can you trust this candidate to put the company first? Is he part of the solution or another potential leaker or whistleblower you have to worry about?

12

QUESTIONS TO DISCOVER
HIDDEN OBJECTIONS

If a candidate has already failed to convince you that her education, experience, competencies, and attitude are what you're seeking, you will probably never ask the questions in this chapter. But if you are still interested, these questions will reveal hidden objections and the extent of each candidate's pre-interview research.

Q: *What do you know about our company?*

What do you want to hear?

Believe it or not, many candidates think this is merely an icebreaker and simply answer "not much." I wouldn't consider this an automatic reason to disqualify an otherwise sterling contender. But I *would* wonder why someone seemingly so captivated by your company and this job (as he's told you, over and over again) would admit to doing no pre-interview research, which indicates to me a total *lack* of interest.

Why would someone go into one of the most important encounters of her life so thoroughly unprepared, then *admit* it?

A successful candidate should have done her homework and welcome this wonderful opportunity to show you how *much* homework she has done.

You probably would like to hear a few salient (and positive) facts about your company, followed, perhaps, by a question that demonstrates real interest. For example:

"Boy, what a growth story Starter Up is! Didn't I read recently that you've had seven straight years of double-digit growth?

"I read in your annual report that you're planning to introduce a new line of products in the near future. I jumped at the chance to apply here. Can you tell me a little bit about this division and the position I'm interviewing for?"

 Thumbs up

Any answer that demonstrates a candidate's pre-interview research. The more informed he is, the more likely you really are at the top of his list of potential employers.

A detailed answer that indicates the breadth of research—from checking out your website to reading your annual report and being familiar with your products and services. Referring to a newspaper, magazine, or online article that mentions the company or, better yet, *you*, is a nice touch, don't you think?

 Thumbs down

A "no" answer followed by a dull stare.

Variations

- What are the important trends you see in our industry?

- Which do you think are our best products or services?

- How do you think our major competitors are doing? And, by the way, who are they?

- What do you know about the community in which we're located?

- In which of our offices would you prefer to work?

- Would you have a problem traveling among a few of our offices?

Q: What interests you most about this position? Our company?

What do you want to hear?

You're probably hoping the candidate has his eye on more responsibility, the opportunity to supervise more people and work at a higher level, and the chance to develop a new set of skills and sharpen the ones he's already acquired. And, of course, if you absolutely *insist* you'll increase his salary, well, he certainly wouldn't say no!

However, this is also the ideal time for a candidate to show what she knows about your company and how the position for which she's interviewing can contribute to its success.

 Thumbs up

Again, a successful candidate should have researched as much as possible about your company, the position, even you, and should take advantage of every opportunity to demonstrate that

191

knowledge. A nice answer might be something like: *"I've heard so much about your titanium ball bearings that I've wanted to experiment with finding different applications for them,"* rather than, *"I'll have a better commute if I get this job."* (Unbelievably, I've heard the latter response from more than one candidate I've interviewed! It may be honest—even very important to the candidate—but it sure wasn't the answer *I* wanted to hear!)

 Thumbs down

Any answer that clearly demonstrates incompatibility. If the candidate's primary interest lies in an area that will be peripheral, at best, to his real function, you can say "thank you, we'll be in touch" and move on to the next applicant. Some previous questions should have identified this mis-qualified candidate earlier, but he or she may have successfully slid by—until now.

Variations

◄ On a scale of one to five, rate your interest in this company. In this job.

◄ Why did you pick us?

Q: *What have you heard about our company that you don't like?*

What do you want to hear?

An intelligent candidate will try to minimize the negative implications of any question, including this one. If there hasn't been any dire news, you should probably expect to hear about the lack of the most recent software or the candidate's wish that the company's profits were a bit more predictable. If the candidate raises a huge negative—*"I'm not sure I like the fact that*

I'll be reporting to three different executives" or "Is it possible to be scheduled for a salary review in 30 days?"—one of you has a problem.

Of course, your interaction will be quite different if there *is* some bad news that needs to be addressed. If your company laid off a significant number of workers months ago, it would be reasonable for a candidate to ask if the dust had settled. If a media report has revealed rumors of your merger with ABC Widget, expect a candidate to know...and ask about them.

Under normal circumstances, you wouldn't expect a candidate to ask questions like this. But you *have* opened the door and invited them, so I'm presuming you really want to know if there's a hidden objection that may impede him or her from accepting your job offer.

Q: Who do you think are our two (or three or five) major competitors?

What do you want to hear?

I encourage asking this question (or one like it) as early in the process as possible. It will quickly and painlessly reveal the depth or shallowness of the candidate's pre-interview research. If the candidate clearly has a handle on your place in the industry and can adequately, even intelligently, discuss your products, your company's strengths and weaknesses, the health of the industry, and so on, you have probably identified a *serious* candidate. Granted, it says absolutely nothing about her particular qualifications for the job, but if she *is* qualified, this display of knowledge may be that "little extra" that separates her (if only in your mind) from other qualified (even slightly *more* qualified) candidates.

Although a lot of hemming, hawing, and nail-biting—along with an obvious lack of an answer—may not lead you to abruptly dismiss the candidate, you should probably consider them warning signs.

Variations

◄ What's our greatest advantage over our competitors?

◄ What's our biggest disadvantage?

◄ Which of our new products do you think has the greatest potential for growth?

◄ What do you think is the greatest challenge facing our company? Our industry?

◄ Which of our products is in trouble?

◄ What do you see as the biggest trend in our industry?

◄ Have you read our most recent annual report?

Q: *This is a much larger (smaller) company than you've worked for. How do you feel about that?*

What do you want to hear?

If your company is larger, the right candidate is undoubtedly looking forward to terrific growth opportunities and exposure to more areas of knowledge than he or she can access now.

If your company is smaller, the candidate is looking forward to a far less bureaucratic organization, in which decisions can be made much more quickly and no department is so large that it is not extremely familiar with the workings of the entire company.

Q: *What are you looking for in your next job?*

What do you want to hear?

Obviously, a savvy interviewee should tailor her response to the job for which she's applying, though answering with a slightly reorganized rendition of the job description isn't the right way to go about it.

Interviewers typically ask a question like this to gauge a candidate's level of interest in the job and see if he has any doubts. A successful candidate should focus on key skills the job requires and emphasize his interest in having a chance to develop (or *further* develop) one of them. Here is an example:

"In my current position as development research associate, I research corporate and government funding opportunities and write grant proposals. I enjoy my work very much, but my contact with prospective donors has been limited.

"I look forward to a position that offers more opportunities to work with donors, securing their support, and ensuring that they are recognized for their contributions.

"I have had a few opportunities to do this with my current employer, and based on my success in dealing with Timely Donations, Inc., I know I can successfully advocate an organization's mission to gain the needed corporate support."

Variations

◄ Describe your ideal job.

◄ If you could have any job in the world, what would it be?

◄ If you could work for any company in the world, which would it be?

Q: *What aspect of the job I've described appeals to you least?*

What do you want to hear?

Let me lead with a little humor. After conversing with his Irish friend one day, a man finally blurted out in consternation, "Why do the Irish always answer a question with a question?" Unruffled, the Irishman winked and replied, "Do we now?"

A heads-up interviewee will do the same:

"You've described a position in which I'd be overseeing some extraordinary levels of output. What sort of quality control procedures does this company have? Will I be able to consult with in-house specialists?"

Much like the question asked earlier (*"What have you heard about our company that you don't like?"*), I'm presuming you're asking this question to *invite* a real answer. If an interviewee you like isn't going to take the job (unbeknownst to you) because of what he or she believes to be a fundamental flaw in the job, you, or the company, you'd want to know about it, wouldn't you?

One of three possible solutions will result:

1. You'll discover an invalid or mistaken objection. Once you answer it, you will again have an interested candidate.

2. You'll discover a viable objection that leads you to eliminate the candidate from consideration.

3. You'll discover a viable objection that will lead the candidate to remove him- or herself from consideration.

Q: Based on what you know about our industry, how does your ideal job stack up against the description of the job for which you're applying?

What do you want to hear?

A viable candidate should use her knowledge about the industry to formulate a reply that, though perhaps a bit idealistic, doesn't sound unrealistic. Here's an example:

"I know that many accounting firms are now deriving more of their fee income from consulting services. I'd like a job that combines my cost-accounting knowledge with client consultation and problem-solving. Ideally, I'd like to start as part of a team, then eventually head up a practice in a specific area, say, cost accounting in manufacturing environments.

"I know this position is in the auditing area and that you hire many of your entry-level people into that department. I must confess I would like this to be a stepping-stone to working more in the manufacturing area and, several years down the line, in consulting. I'm sure I don't have the requisite knowledge or experience yet. Is this a position in which I can gain such experience, and is this a career track that's possible at this firm?"

Q: How will you handle the least interesting or most unpleasant parts of this job?

What do you want to hear?

If you plan to pose this question, you will probably want to build in specific aspects of the position, such as: "You won't always be looking for creative solutions to our clients' tax problems. Most of the time, you'll be preparing returns and ensuring they comply with the latest laws. You're aware of that, of course?"

You would expect a positive response like this:

"I'm sure that every job in the accounting field has its routine tasks. They have to be done, too. Doing those tasks is part of the satisfaction of doing the job well. They make the relatively infrequent chances we have to be creative even more satisfying."

Q: You've had little experience with budgeting (or sales or whatever). How do you intend to learn what you need to know to perform on this job?

What do you want to hear?

Depending on the job opening and the state of employment in your industry or region, you can't assume you will always (or easily) find a candidate with the pertinent experience you desire.

You may even prefer to "grow" an entry-level person into a professional position. In either case, you will want to be convinced—through deeds, not just words—that a candidate has the wherewithal to learn what he or she needs to within a realistic time frame. Here's a good answer to this question:

"Well, throughout my career, I've proven to be a quick study. For example, when my company's inventory system was computerized, I didn't have the time to go through the training. But the company that supplied the software had developed some computer-based tutorials and training manuals. I studied them and practiced at home. I hope that I'd be able to do something similar to pick up the rudiments of your budgeting system."

Q: How long do you plan to stay with us?

What do you want to hear?

One answer I *don't* want to hear is "forever," because I simply won't believe it (and I'd wonder about the intelligence of a candidate who thinks I would). You should expect a fairly simple answer along the lines of "as long as I continue to grow, learn, and contribute in ways you feel are valuable."

I'm not sure whether this question will ever give you any useful information, because any candidate saying *"Oh, a month or two, until I find a job I really like"* shouldn't have made it through your screening process (or, for that matter, the first two or three interview questions). But if you watch someone very closely when you ask this question, body language will often give you just the information you require! Squirming or fidgeting *does* seem to imply *"Oh, a month or two, until I find a job I really like!"*

If the candidate already appears to be a job-hopper but gives you the standard "as long as I continue to grow" speech, ask, *"Is that what you told the interviewers at your four previous positions?"* It will be interesting to see how he or she responds, especially if the answer is, *"Yes, actually, and they all believed me, too!"*

Q: *How do you think I've handled this interview?*

What do you want to hear?

Well, now, what is the poor candidate to do? Saying "lousy" doesn't seem appropriate, but "Great, sir, may I have another?" seems a bit too obsequious. There is no right answer, but it will be interesting to see how much he squirms and how rapidly he tries to ask a question of his own to get you off this track.

Of course, if a candidate has already decided she's not interested in the job, you might hear some criticisms that will actually make you a better interviewer. So I would only ask this question if you really want to hear an honest answer.

Q: *Do you have any questions?*

What do you want to hear?

Although many candidates ask questions as an interview progresses—and you may or may not encourage such deviations from your formal or informal script—it's always a good idea to give all candidates the time to do so. But I strongly urge you to prepare for the detailed questions some candidates will be ready to hurl at you. You may need to research your own company a bit (and think long and hard about the job description) to prepare for the most inquisitive candidates.

Following is a list of questions a candidate should have tried getting the answers to *before* the interview. Notice that I said "tried." Not all such information will be easily obtainable, especially if you're a small, privately held company.

So, as part of *your* preparation, presume that a good candidate will be asking *you* some of these questions:

Questions about your company

◄ Do you have a lot of employees working flextime or telecommuting?

◄ How many employees work for the organization? In how many offices? In this office?

◄ Is the company planning to grow through acquisitions?

◄ Is there anything else you feel it is vital I know about the company (or department or job)?

◄ Please tell me about your own tenure with the company.

◄ What are the company's key markets, and are those markets growing?

- ◄ What are the company's plans and prospects for growth and expansion?

- ◄ What are your leading products or services? What products or services is it planning to introduce in the near future?

- ◄ What do *you* like best about this company? Why?

- ◄ What do you see as key goals for the company during the next year?

- ◄ What growth rate are you currently anticipating? Will this be accomplished internally or through acquisitions?

- ◄ What has been the company's layoff history in the last five years? Do you anticipate any cutbacks in the near future? If you do, how will they impact my department or position?

- ◄ What is your hiring philosophy?

- ◄ What is your ranking within the industry? Does this represent a change from where it was a year or a few years ago?

- ◄ What major problems or challenges has the company recently faced? How were they addressed? What results do you expect?

- ◄ Which other companies serving your markets pose a serious threat?

- ◄ Who owns the company?

- ◄ Will you be entering any new markets in the next couple of years? Which ones and via what kind of distribution channel(s)?

Questions about the department or division

◄ Are there specific challenges you are facing right now?

◄ Can you explain the organizational structure of the department and its primary functions and responsibilities?

◄ How is the department's performance measured?

◄ How many people work exclusively in this department?

◄ To whom will I be reporting? To whom does my boss report?

◄ What are its current goals and objectives?

◄ What are the department's strengths and weaknesses?

◄ What has the turnover been in the last couple of years?

◄ What is its budget? Who is part of the planning process?

◄ What would you most like to see changed in this department?

◄ With which other departments does this department work most closely?

Questions about the job

◄ Can you give me a better idea of the kinds of decisions I could make (or amounts I could spend) without oversight?

◄ Could you describe a typical day in this position?

◄ Does this job usually lead to other positions in the company? Which ones?

◄ How advanced or current is the hardware and software I will be expected to use?

◄ How did this job become available? Was the previous person promoted? What is his or her new title?

◄ Was the previous person fired? Why?

◄ How do you see my role evolving in the first two years?

◄ How long has this position been available?

◄ How many people will be reporting to me?

◄ How much budgetary responsibility will I have?

◄ How much day-to-day autonomy will I have?

◄ How much travel should I expect in a typical month?

◄ Is a written job description available?

◄ Is relocation an option, a possibility, or a requirement?

◄ Is there anyone within the organization who is interviewing for this position?

◄ On what basis are raises and bonuses awarded?

◄ Please tell me a little bit about the people with whom I'll be working most closely.

◄ What do you think my biggest challenge will be?

◄ What is the first problem I should tackle?

◄ What kind of training should I expect and for how long?

◄ What three things need immediate attention?

◄ Would I be able to speak with the person who held this job previously?

You should be very close to separating the candidates you want to hire from those you should have sent home an hour ago. In the next chapter, I'll make sure you know what questions you *shouldn't* ask, then explore the final "wrap-up" questions, some of which you may want to intersperse much earlier in the interview process (and I'll tell you why).

13

AVOIDING ILLEGAL QUESTIONS

In an age dominated by social media, it is easier than ever for you to glean information about candidates that you would normally not be allowed to ask about. How old are they? Well, you can certainly do the math if their resume says they graduated high school in 2010. And if their Facebook page features a visit to Pakistan to "see family and friends," you may no longer wonder about their national origin.

But just because such information may be readily available doesn't mean you can ask about it during an interview. There is a long list of questions (and variations) you should avoid asking. If you are a human resources professional, you are undoubtedly aware of them. If you are not, this chapter may keep you out of trouble. Do not ask the following questions:

Questions about age

◄ How old are you?

◄ When were you born?

◄ When did you graduate from high school?

◄ When did you graduate from college?

◄ Are you near retirement age?

◄ Aren't you a little young to be seeking a job with this much responsibility?

◄ Aren't you a little too old for a fast-changing company like ours?

Questions about marital status and family

◄ Are you single, married, separated, or divorced?

◄ What do you think caused your divorce?

◄ Why have you never married?

◄ Were you ever married?

◄ Do you intend to marry?

◄ Do you live alone?

◄ Do you have any children?

◄ What was your maiden name?

◄ Is that the last name you were born with?

◄ Do you prefer to be called Miss, Ms., or Mrs.?

◄ Are you a single parent?

◄ How many dependents are you responsible for?

◄ Who's the boss in your family?

- What kind of work does your spouse do?
- How much time do you spend with your family?
- Tell me about your children.
- Do you have a good relationship with your children?
- Do you have any children not living with you?
- Do you live with your parents?
- What childcare arrangements have you made for your children?
- My darn kids seem to pick up every bug that comes around. Yours, too?
- My wife (husband) hates me working on weekends. What about yours?
- Do you practice birth control?
- Are you pregnant?
- Do you intend to have children?
- Will travel be a burden on your family?
- Are you a family man (woman)?

Q: How do you manage to balance career and family?

What do you want to hear?

This is a perfectly legal question, but it does make it decidedly difficult for a candidate who is determined to keep any discussion of family out of the interview. Why would she want to avoid such a discussion? She may worry that you have some unwritten rules, such as no single parents hired for travel positions (or, for that matter, no parents if travel is excessive), and she doesn't want to lose the chance at the job because of them.

Accordingly, a candidate attempting to give an answer that is as unrevealing as possible may try something like this:

"I have been a dedicated, loyal, and hard-working employee throughout my career and nothing in my personal life—family obligations, hobbies, or volunteer work—has ever affected my performance. Nor would I ever expect it to."

Questions about ethnic origin

◄ What's your nationality?

◄ Hmm, that's a ___ (Italian, Greek, etc.) name, isn't it?

◄ What language do you speak at home?

◄ Where are your parents from?

◄ Where were you born?

◄ Where were your parents born?

◄ What languages do your parents speak?

◄ Were your parents born in this country?

◄ Were you born in this country?

◄ What kind of accent is that?

◄ What languages do you speak?*

◄ Are you bilingual?*

* These last two are legal questions if proficiency in one or more foreign languages is a requirement of the job.

Questions about sexual preference

◄ What's your sexual orientation?

◄ Are you straight?

◄ Are you gay?

◄ Are you a lesbian?

◄ Do you date other men?

◄ Do you date other women?

◄ Do you have any roommates?

◄ Do you live with anyone?

◄ Do you belong to any gay or lesbian groups?

◄ What gender is your spouse?

◄ Do you identify with the gender on your birth certificate?

◄ Are you gender fluid?

Questions about religious preference

◄ Are you ___ (Jewish, Christian, Buddhist, etc.)?

◄ What do you do Sunday mornings?

◄ Can you work Friday evenings?

◄ We're a ___ (Christian, Jewish, Muslim) firm. Would that be a problem for you?

◄ Are you a member of any religious group?

◄ What religion do you practice?

◄ What religious group do you belong to?

◄ Do you tithe?

◄ Are you "born again"?

◄ Do your children go to Sunday School?

◄ Do your children go to Hebrew School?

- Do your children attend a madrassa?
- Do you sing in the church choir?
- What church do you belong to?
- What temple do you regularly attend?
- What mosque do you regularly attend?
- Is there any day of the week on which you can't work?
- Will working on weekends be a problem for you?
- What religious holidays will you need to take?
- Have you ever done any missionary work?

Questions about health and disabilities

- Do you have any physical problems?
- Do you have any health problems?
- How many days were you sick last year?
- Do you spend a lot on prescriptions?
- Can you read the fine print on this form?
- How's your back?
- Is your hearing good?
- Are you physically fit?
- Were you ever denied health insurance?
- Were you ever denied life insurance?
- When were you last in the hospital?
- When did you last consult a doctor?

- ◄ Do you have a doctor you see regularly?
- ◄ Are you handicapped?
- ◄ Have you ever filed a worker's compensation claim?
- ◄ Are you sensitive about your weight?
- ◄ Are you on a diet?
- ◄ Shouldn't you be on a diet?

Q: *What organizations do you belong to?*

You should legitimately be interested in a candidate's membership in organizations, professional societies, or other associations considered important to his or her performance on the job. But you should not ask about organizations in an effort to identify a candidate's race, religious creed, color, national origin, ancestry, gender, or disability.

Q: *Have you ever gone bankrupt?*

You may ask what the candidate is currently earning (and what he or she hopes to be paid by you), but current or past assets, liabilities, or credit ratings are not fair game. This includes whether he or she owns a home or any information about a past bankruptcy or garnishment of wages (except when permitted by federal and state laws governing credit-related information). You should consult specific guidelines in your state.

Variations

- ◄ Do you own or rent your home?
- ◄ Do you have any outside income?
- ◄ Do you earn any money from hobbies or investments?

Q: *What was your record in the military?*

A candidate who served in the military may choose to highlight the relevant skills and knowledge he or she gained from that experience, but he or she is not required to give the dates of military service or the type of discharge received.

Variations

◄   What kind of discharge did you receive from the military?

Q: *Have you ever been arrested?*

Unless someone is applying for a position as a police officer or with the Department of Justice, you are not entitled to know whether a candidate has been arrested, unless the arrest resulted in a conviction.

In some states, you may only ask about felonies, not misdemeanors. But regulations differ from state to state and from industry to industry. For example, under the Federal Deposit Insurance Act, banks are prohibited from hiring individuals convicted of any crime involving dishonesty or breach of trust, even if the conviction is more than seven years old.

~~~

To be clear, I am not an attorney and this chapter should not be considered legal advice.

If you are unsure whether or not a question is discriminatory, check with your company's legal department or outside counsel. Given the current nature of our litigious society, "better safe than sorry" might mean "better still in business than bankrupt."

14

Wrap It Up

Even if you are convinced you identified your ideal candidate quite a few questions (or chapters) ago, there are some final details to confirm. Here are the questions to ask to lock in your new hire:

Q: *Is there anything else about you I should know?*

What do you want to hear?

Even if you're both exhausted, a good candidate will treat this question like a lifeline (and as a sign that you're trying to wrap things up) and, once again, summarize the reasons why he, and only he, is the right one for the job:

"Mr. Krueger, I think we've covered everything. But I want to re-emphasize the key strengths that I would bring to this position:

"Experience: The job I'm currently in is quite similar to this one, and I would be excited by the chance to apply what I've learned at BG Industries to working for you.

"Management skills: I run a department almost equal in size to this one. I'm a fair and effective supervisor.

"A record of success: I've won two prestigious industry awards. I would bring that creativity to TCI.

"Enthusiasm: I am very excited about the prospect of working with you here at TCI Ltd. When do you expect to make a decision?"

Variations

◄ Why should I hire you?

◄ If you were me, would you hire you?

Q: *What salary are you expecting?*

What do you want to hear?

Well, I suspect you'd love to hear something like, "Golly, this job sounds so gosh-darned wonderful I can't believe you're going to pay me anything! Just give me an office and a phone and I'll work for the sheer fun of it!"

And pigs will be flying to the moon tonight.

This is another question that we've left until the end of the book but you may well want to ask very early on. When I ran a relatively small ($5 million) company, cash flow was a constant nemesis and affording good people was a major challenge. So this question was often the first or second asked by the screening interviewer, because it didn't matter how wonderful the candidate was if he or she wanted twice what we could afford. Even if you've clearly indicated a salary range in an ad or post, some people will have no problem asking for double what you are authorized to offer.

The less leeway you have to adjust salary according to experience, the more likely you'll want to ask this question early. But be careful—an experienced interviewee will do everything but jump out the window before being sucked into a salary discussion, knowing full well that his value will only increase as the interview goes on.

A successful candidate will avoid committing herself to a specific number and, instead, cite a range: "I believe a fair wage for this kind of position would be between $32,000 and $35,000." It should be assumed that the bottom end of that range is the minimum salary that the applicant would be willing to accept.

Variations

◄ What do you think you should be paid?

◄ What are you worth?

◄ How much do you want (expect) to make?

◄ What are your salary expectations?

◄ How much were you paid last year?

◄ If I'm going to make you an offer, I want to ensure it is competitive. What will it take?

Q: *The salary you're asking for is near the top of the range for this job. Why should we pay you this much?*

What do you want to hear?

You expect the candidate to justify the higher money, citing all of the factors—accomplishments, experience, skills, and so on—that you should consider before hiring him or her. A candidate may just take an entirely different approach and jump right to the bottom line:

"I was able to cut my previous employer's expenses by 10 percent by negotiating better deals with vendors. I think it's reasonable to expect that any additional salary we agree to would be offset by savings I could bring the company."

Variations

◄ Why are you asking to be paid so little?

◄ Are you willing to take a pay cut to work here?

◄ Are you willing to start at a salary less than you made on your last job?

◄ Do you think you were overpaid at your last position?

◄ Do you have a problem working regular overtime?

Q: Is there anything that will inhibit you from taking this job if offered?

What do you want to hear?

"Absolutely not."

You are attempting to do everything in your power to ascertain whether this person will accept the job if offered and actually show up on the start date. But there is no way you can guarantee either. All you can hope to do is give the candidate another opportunity to voice a previously hidden concern: too small a salary, a poor benefits package, a lousy cubicle, reporting to too many people, inadequate support, unrealistic sales or profit expectations, and so on.

Variation

◄ If I made you a great offer right now, would you accept on the spot?

Q: *Are you considering any other offers right now?*

What do you want to hear?

This is another "closing" question I like to ask early in the process so I know what I'm up against. Some of you will want to hear "no," so you feel secure (perhaps unwisely) that the candidate will accept your job if offered. Others will actually welcome a positive response, believing that anyone who is already wanted by other companies—maybe even your competition—is a more attractive candidate.

Of course, this is presuming that you expect an honest answer, which, frankly, is less than likely. Unless he thinks you will respond positively to such an admission, a savvy candidate will attempt to play his cards very close to the vest. He probably gains nothing by admitting he has other irons in the fire, so why stir up the coals?

Variations

◄   Tell me about the other offers you're considering.

◄   How does this job compare to others for which you are interviewing?

◄   How does the offer I've made compare to others you have received?

Q: *Is there anything in the package I've offered you that we need to discuss?*

What do you want to hear?

If a candidate has questions about the reporting structure, workload, or job responsibilities, she will probably feel little compunction to hide her concerns. But money is an issue few people like to talk about. So even if she feels she's going to be underpaid, she may be hesitant to discuss it. Or you may have given the impression that there is little to negotiate. So if the candidate has a slightly better offer in her hip pocket, you may lose her, *even if you would have been willing to increase your offer to beat the competition.* In other words, what you don't know can indeed hurt you, so it is in *your* best interest to give the candidate every opportunity to admit, after much cajoling, that another thousand dollars would lock her up.

Variation

◄ What benefits are most important to you?

Q: *When can you start?*

What do you want to hear?

If the candidate has been laid off or fired, you would expect he or she could start immediately, of course.

If the candidate is still working for someone else, you would expect him to give at least two weeks' notice to his current employer—more if he is leaving a position in which he has considerable responsibility. Wouldn't you want that kind of consideration if he were leaving you?

Because this is the last or very near the last question you might ask, if there is any possibility that the candidate isn't sure, it had better surface now. Just be careful: Do *not* assume that the candidate is ready and willing to go ahead just because she agrees to a start date. If you've been interviewing people for a few years, I'm sure you've had supposed hires simply not show up on the agreed-upon start date, without even the courtesy of a phone call. But if you've conducted the interview properly and used a couple of the closing questions discussed earlier, you may lessen the odds of staring at a pile of paperwork and an empty desk waiting for your new assistant.

Most interviewees assume, especially if this question has been left to the very end, that they are hired, or at least very close to hired. I suggest you ask this question quite *early* in the process to get some pertinent information right from the start. (You can start tomorrow? What happened to your last position? Only need to give a week's notice? What will your current employer think?)

 **Thumbs up**

A candidate who says he can't start for three or four weeks because he wants to help his current employer find and train his replacement. It may be longer than you'd like to wait, but I personally would love to be introduced to someone who is that responsible!

If a candidate cannot start for several weeks—whatever the reason—I would consider it a plus if she offered to begin studying literature or files in her off-hours. Or come into the office in the evening or on a weekend or two to meet members of the staff and begin to familiarize herself with the lay of the land.

 Thumbs down

A person who "isn't sure" about when she can start. Because a candidate with a positive attitude would have *assumed* she was going to land the job, why wouldn't she be ready to answer the obvious question about a starting date? As far as I'm concerned, what she isn't saying is that she "isn't sure" about taking the job.

A candidate who can't start for several weeks because he wants to take a vacation. I can empathize with someone who feels the need to recover from a bitter job experience before punching the clock at a new one, but there's just something that sticks in my craw about such an answer. Perhaps it's feeling that the new hire is already putting his own needs above mine—maybe it's a real hardship for me to wait four weeks. Maybe it's my own idiosyncrasy, but I *really* hate to hear about someone planning a vacation before starting to work for me.

~~~

You've done it—sifted through hundreds of resumes, done a dozen or more screening interviews, brought in six viable candidates for in-person interviews, and, finally, chosen one. You know whom you're ready to hire.

If you've asked the right questions and used the information the candidate offered in reply to construct an increasingly detailed array of follow-up questions, you may just have landed the right person for the job!

The last step is to phone or email the candidate to make a final offer, give him or her a reasonable period in which to respond (at least two days, no more than a week), then confirm all pertinent details in writing.

You may or may not send a brief, professional letter or email to each candidate you did not hire.

Congratulations!

Index

Adaptation, 128-129

Age, questions about, 206

Anticipating problems, 132-133

Arrests, 212

Attire, 9

Attitude, 126

Bankruptcy, 211

Behavioral interview, 38-39

Blame, 31-32

Body language, 11, 49, 50-52

Books, questions about, 62

Brainteaser interview, 46

Breathing, 52

Business Etiquette, 59

Business style, 125-138

Candidates, entry-level, 93

Candidates' questions, 201-203

Career advancement, 175

Case interview, 42-43

Change, 128-129

Checking references, 10

Chemistry, 70

Clarifying questions, 77

Code of ethics, personal, 186

Collaboration, 142

Communication skills, 185-186

Communication, 141

Competencies, 40-41, 139-155

Competency-based
    interview, 39-41

Competency-Based Interviews,
    39, 53, 141

Confidence, 22, 27, 30, 31, 82, 95

Conflict, 135-136

Conversational questions, 63

Core competencies, 139-155

Corporate culture, 20-21

Creativity, 43, 133, 142

Criticism from supervisors, 174

Crossed arms, 52

Decision-making, 129-131

Defining the job, 15-25

Delegation, 126, 139, 177

Demotions, 159

Dependability, 22, 27, 30, 31, 95

Disabilities, questions about, 210-211

Discovering hidden objections, 189-204

Discrimination, 34

Economic environment, the, 5

Education, 93-105

Energy, 95

Enthusiasm, 22, 27, 30, 31, 76, 95

Entry-level candidates, 93

Errors on resumes, 24

Ethical standards, 137-138

Ethics, personal code of, 186

Ethnic origin, questions about, 208

Executives, questions for, 177-187

Expectations, salary, 214-216

Experience, 22, 27, 30, 31, 42

Extracurricular activities, 94-97

Eye contact, 11, 50, 51, 75

Failure, 89-90, 114-116

False sense of security, 63

Family, questions about, 206-207

Financial responsibility, 148-149

Flexibility, 124, 142

Focus, 141

Follow-up interview, 46-47

Format, interview, 37

Frequent job changes, 10-123

Frustration, 131

Future reactions, 38

Future, 80-81

Generalities, 55-56

Good interviewing, 6

Grammatical errors, 24

Green, Paul, 39

Greeting, 50

Grooming, 52

Growth, opportunities for, 158

Handshake, 50

Health, 67

    questions about, 210-212

Heroes, 61-62

Hidden objections, 189-204

Hobbies, 65-67

Honesty, 95

Humility, 79

Hygiene, 52

Icebreaker questions, 49, 60

Illegal questions, 14, 31, 205-212

Inconsistencies, 163

Inexperience, 70

Influence, 142

Initial greeting, 50

Innovation, 133, 142

Insecurity, 52

Integrity, 138

Interests, 65-66

Internships, 102

Interpersonal awareness, 142

Interview

    format, 37

    outline, written, 47

Interview, screening, 27-35

Interviewing, good, 6

Interviews, types of, 7, 37-48

Irrelevant job components, 18

Job changes, frequent, 122-124

Job components, irrelevant, 18

Job descriptions, 7

Job search, length of, 164-165

Job,
defining the, 15-25
most recent, 157-176
Judgment, 6
Kessler, Robin, 39, 41, 53, 141
Key competencies, 40-41
Language, professional, 75-76
Lateness, 54-55
Lateral moves, 108, 159
Layoffs, 160-161
Leadership, 118
Length of job search, 164-165
Length of responses, 52
Life-work balance, 207-208
Listening, 49
Loyalty, 124
Lying, 10, 25, 53, 54, 132, 186-187
Management philosophy, 125,
177-178
Managers, questions for, 177-187
Managing people, 117-118
Marital status, questions about,
206-207
Military record, 212
Mistakes, 139
Most recent job, 157-176
Motivating others, 119-120
Motivation, 141
Movies, 63-64
Needs assessment, 126
Negative interview, 45
Negativity, 31-32, 111, 112,
158, 161
Nerves, 69, 76
Nonverbal communication, 11,
49, 54

Objections, discovering hidden,
189-204
Observation, 49
Open-ended questions, 28
Opportunities for growth, 158
Organization, 126-127
Outline, written interview, 47
Overqualified candidates, 58-59
People, managing, 117-118
Perfection, 39
Performance appraisals, 171
Personal
code of ethics, 186
credibility, 142
Positivity, 11, 74, 75
Posture, 51, 52
Practical experience, 42
Preparation, 12, 15, 20, 70, 71,
189-191, 193-194
Pressure, 131-132
Probing questions, 28, 132,
137, 143, 181
Problems, anticipating, 132-133
Problem-solving, 140
Procrastination, 127
Productivity, 83
Professional language, 75-76
Project management, 126
Promotions, 108
Questions
about age, 206
about disabilities, 210-211
about ethnic origin, 208
about family, 206-207
about health, 210-212
about marital status, 206-207

about religious preference, 209-210
about sexual preference, 208-209
for managers, 177-187
for managers/executives, 177-187
from candidates, 200-203
that aren't questions, 28-29
to discover hidden objections, 189-204
Questions,
  illegal, 14, 31, 205-212
  open-ended, 28
  rapport-building, 28, 51
  throwaway, 49
Rapport-building questions, 28, 50
Reactions, future, 38
Reading, 62
References, 10, 32, 146
Regrets, 133-134
Relevance, 76
Religious preference, questions about, 209-210
Relocation, 68
Responsibility, 115, 158
Responsibility, financial, 148-149
Revolving door positions, 17
Risk, 133
Sabath, Ann Marie, 59
Salary expectations, 214-216
Screening interview, 27-35
Security, false sense of, 63
Self-confidence, 142
Sexual preference, questions about, 208-209
Silence, 57
Situational interview, 43-44
Smiling, 50, 51
Social media, 64-65, 205
Start date, 218-220
Strengths, 79
Stress interview, 44-45
Stress, 131, 142
Style, business, 125-138
Success, 87
Supervisors, criticism from, 175
Team interview, 41
Teamwork, 141
Thinking processes, 42
Throwaway questions, 49
Time management, 126, 127-128
Timing of responses, 52
Tone of responses, 52
Tone of voice, 49, 53
Travel, 67-68
Types of interviews, 7, 37-48
Typographic errors, 24
Underqualified candidates, 58-59
Unemployment, 7
Unimportant questions, 61
Values, 42
Verbal timing, 49
Vocal delivery, 54
Weaknesses, 74, 116
White lies, 132
Work experience, 107-124
Worker's compensation, 211
Written interview outline, 47